ATOMIC BRANDING

How to win business and influence colleagues
with your authentic personal brand

CRAIG ROBBINS

Atomic Branding. Copyright © 2023–2024 by Craig Robbins

All rights reserved. This book or any portion thereof may not be reproduced in any form or used in any manner whatsoever without the express written permission of the publisher, except for the use of brief quotations in a book review. All images in this book, with the exception of famous company logos used for educational purposes only, are original to this book.

Second printing, March 2024
Nonfiction: Business: Motivation & self-improvement; Entrepreneurship; Career success & career guides; Communication skills.

Atomic Branding provides marketing and branding theory and a step-by-step process to define an individual's personal brand in business. The workbook includes case studies and exercises to aid in personal branding self-discovery, connection to a target market, delivery, and refinement of the brand.

For information, address:
Craig Robbins
www.CraigRobbinsNextLevel.com

Credits:
Author: Craig Robbins
Developmental & line editor: Heidi Tretheway
Contributor: Katherine E. E. Steen
Copy editor: Cynthia Moyer
Formatting: Moyer & Tretheway
Cover design & interior images: Tretheway

WHAT PEOPLE ARE SAYING

"I have been teaching personal branding for 20-plus years and sometimes I fall into the trap of thinking I know all there is to know on the subject. Wrong! Atomic Branding was a great wake-up call that there is always more to learn. It **demystifies and walks you through the process of selecting the right personal brand** for you. For me, the most powerful principle is: If you don't manage your brand, someone else will ... unless they don't think of you at all. Ouch!"

— Tim O'Brien, President, The Personal Branding Group, Inc.

"Craig and I have worked together for over 20 years, and together we grew a $280 million local real estate franchise into a $2.5 billion global player. Craig's coaching was not only responsible for our exceptional growth as an organization, but his unique insight, ideas and techniques have had an amazing impact on my personal life as well. Working with Craig is not for the faint of heart. But if you are willing to be pushed, and can look at yourself and your business objectively, **there is no better way to separate yourself from the pack**."

— Doug Frye, Board Member, Cauze;
former CEO, Colliers International

"This book is a game-changer. Craig's coaching on this subject has **accelerated my career by over a decade**. It helped me find and articulate my identity so clearly that it's known and repeated while I'm not in the room. Not to mention, I've been able to differentiate myself in a highly competitive industry and transact at a speed and in quantities that I didn't even know were possible."

— Renee Castillo, Advisory & Transaction Services, CBRE

"Craig's coaching **expedited my career and led to closing several of my largest clients**. His guidance and expertise will take anyone to the next level."

— David Tassone, MBA, CFP, Principal, Solidi Wealth Advisors

"The training will change the way you look at life and how you interact with people. Craig **helped me to rebrand myself in my business and showed me how to effectively communicate differently with my customers**. His training led to my largest sales number to start my goal for 2020. We achieved over 40% of my sales goal in the first sales month of year."

— Justin Bose, Sales Executive, James P. Bennett & Company

"Some of the best coaches were also great players! If you are willing to invest and be coached, **you can never go wrong by working with someone that has a proven track record as a top performer**. Craig clearly articulates how to define your Atomic Brand with great examples and quick tasks that can prove to be challenging, but very well worth it."

— Stefano Desanti, Managing Principal, The Tenant Advisors

"I'm only halfway through this book and **already I feel as though I've got knowledge 100x worth what I paid for it**. Robbins takes complex ideas and simplifies them to actionable concepts while providing **potent examples of the giants in various industries who have expertly branded themselves**. There are two ideas here: discovering yourself so you can be more of that, or creating yourself so you can serve a purpose that fulfills you."

— Kyle E. Guerrero, musician

"This book is incredibly valuable to me — everyone can develop and build their personal brand with Craig Robbins' teachings, which he has used for years and only now has made available with this first published work. It explains the importance of having such a brand, how to find yours, develop it, and use it in business and the workplace. It contains many exercises to help you generate your brand by identifying your approach, passion, and experiences. He then **helps you connect your brand to your "customer" by refining your offer and value**."

— Brad Bredemann, CFA, Vice President,
PRIMECAP Management Company

"How can you be successful without knowing who you are and what you offer? How can you teach people to relay the correct information about you? How can you add value in a specialized world? How can you stand out? This book answers all of that and more. **This is not just a business book. It's a book about life. This book removes your need to rely on chance and throws "it's a numbers game" out the window.**"

— Bill Froelich, Vice Chair, Colliers International

"**Read this book multiple times because there were that many takeaways**. The author is intentional and deliberate about the fundamentals and key factors of impactful branding. Branding is the core of every successful business. Many principles in this book have become the foundation of my business and will continue be…"

— Nathan Fong, Executive Vice President,
Retail, Hotel & Investment, Colliers International

Contents

1	**Introduction**
2	Everyone has a personal brand
2	Why you need this book
3	What do I get when I get you?
5	Why me?
7	How to use this book
9	**Chapter 1: Why bother with branding?**
10	The very, very, very first thing to know about branding
11	First principles for branding
12	It's not who you know
13	Stereotype vs. brand
15	Case study: From bigwig to nobody
15	Snap judgments
16	Case study: Dress for success
17	Got commoditized milk?
21	**Chapter 2: What is a brand?**
22	Name that brand
22	Exercise 2.1: Name that company based on its logo
23	Exercise 2.2: Name that company based on its tagline
23	What's in a brand?
25	Elements of a brand
26	Putting it into practice
27	Definition: Market identity
28	Definition: Market position
29	Definition: Approach
30	Case study: One job, four approaches
31	Definition: Value proposition
32	How do you differentiate a brand?
32	Definition: Target audience or market

33	Definition: Experience
34	Case study: Pancakes at the Waffle House
34	Definition: Product position
35	Definition: Pricing
37	Let's make branding personal
39	Exercise 2.3: What are these brands known for?
39	What a brand isn't
40	Why can't you differentiate on some things?
41	Why a slogan isn't a brand
41	How do you differentiate from competitors?
45	**Chapter 3: Branding a person**
46	What is personal branding?
47	What's the difference between brand and reputation?
48	Case study: Embracing clients' concerns
49	Why your personal brand matters
50	Case study: Saying no to things outside your offer
51	Your personal brand is pure you
52	Show them your personal brand
54	Case study: What if a promotion isn't a good fit?
54	Your personal brand doesn't have to be nice
55	Your personal brand doesn't have to be job-specific
55	Case study: A negative brand can work, too
56	Choosing your personal brand
57	Case study: From bookkeeper to creative writer
57	Why your passion for 1980s punk rock matters
58	Exercise 3.1: Other people's brands
59	Exercise 3.2: First impressions
59	Exercise 3.3: Are you consistent?
60	Case study: Using your passion to find your purpose
61	What's not your personal brand?
62	Something else you should know about your personal brand
63	You can change how the market views you
63	Case study: Keep pressing for the right opportunity
64	Exercise 3.4: Brevity is key
65	Make it snappy
66	Why brand matters to potential clients and customers
67	Key elements of your personal brand
67	Case study: Using a natural approach to benefit the client
68	Exercise 3.5: Your big billboard

71	**Chapter 4: Generating your personal brand**
72	Control it, or it controls you
74	Case study: Partners with different strengths
75	Case study: Using a personal brand for career growth
76	Key elements of your approach
77	How do you approach your role?
77	Definition: Thinkers
77	Definition: Analyzers
78	Definition: Do-ers
78	Definition: Intuits
79	Exercise 4.1: What's your dominant approach?
80	Exercise 4.2: Make it an action
81	Exercise 4.3: Discovering your action phrase
82	Alternative exercise 4.4: Building your glossary
86	Alternative exercise 4.5: Finding your theme
87	Alternative exercise 4.6: Narrowing it down
88	The missing words
90	Case study: Fuji vs. Kodak
90	Exercise 4.7: "I'm your go-to person for …"
91	What's in it for me?
92	Exercise 4.8: Make yourself commercial
94	Case study: My self-discovery exercise
95	Case study: A brand without a reason to transact
95	Exercise 4.9: For the sake of …
98	Case study: Owning your approach
99	Why describing your approach is not enough
101	**Chapter 5: Your approach is not enough without passion**
102	Passion gives your life, and life gives you passion
103	Share the love
103	What if you don't have a passion?
105	Exercise 5.1: Finding your passions
105	Exercise 5.2: Doing your passions
107	Case study: Connecting your passion to your vocation
108	Be a willing learner
109	The difference between approach and intention
111	Exercise 5.3: Where do you spend your time?

113	**Chapter 6: To the résumé — and beyond!**
114	Taking your inventory
115	Your qualifications
115	Capabilities
117	Case study: Finding a unique selling point
118	Exercise 6.1: Discovering your capabilities
120	Credibility and credentials
121	Exercise 6.2: Discovering your credentials
122	Case study: Lessons that weave through a career
124	You're qualified. So what?
125	Exercise 6.3: Your unique experiences
126	Exercise 6.4: Create your own commercial
129	Exercise 6.5: Fill in the blanks
129	Case study: Reframing your value to pique interest
130	Applying Atomic Brand rules
130	What is your Atomic Brand? (Defining it)
131	How does your Atomic Brand grow? (Managing it)
133	**Chapter 7: Connecting with your audience**
134	Client discovery
136	How do you pick clients who value what you offer?
137	Exercise 7.1: Who knows your approach?
138	Exercise 7.2: Discovering your target audience
140	Exercise 7.3: Narrowing your target audience
142	Features and benefits
143	Case study: Is handmade a feature, benefit, or neither?
144	Exercise 7.4: Identifying the benefits to your target audience
146	Exercise 7.5: Telling your target audience
149	Case study: When clients have different needs
150	Exercise 7.6: Adapting your commercial to your target audience
151	Case study: Don't just ask for any job, focus on the benefit to them
152	Another way to identify your target audience

153	The influence and familiarity grid
154	Exercise 7.7: Filling Box 1
156	Exercise 7.8: Filling Box 2
157	Exercise 7.9: Filling Box 3
158	Case study: Referral by accident
158	Exercise 7.10: Filling Box 4
159	Exercise 7.11: Linking them all together
159	Exercise 7.12: Applying your domain
160	Exercise 7.13: Your priority contacts
161	Case study: Shifting your focus to clients who value what you offer
162	Putting it all together
162	Exercise 7.14: What's your offer again?
163	Exercise 7.15: Refining your offer
164	The offer and value conversation
165	Case study: Don't assume what matters most to the client
166	The power of your stories
166	Exercise 7.16: What's your story?
169	**Chapter 8: Making empathy part of your process**
170	What is empathy?
171	How to use and practice empathy
172	Case study: Over-deliver for the person, not just the business
173	Overcoming the language barrier
175	Exercise 8.1: Using their language
177	**Chapter 9: Finding your perfect fit**
178	The right fit for you
181	Exercise 9.1: How your brand fits in
182	Exercise 9.2: What's your theme?
184	Exercise 9.3: Finessing the fit
185	Exercise 9.4: Where do you want to fit?
185	Case study: Does your audience really want your offer?
186	Exercise 9.5: Finding where you want to fit
188	Case study: Defining your target

191	**Chapter 10: Access and action**
192	Access your target audience
194	Exercise 10.1: Reaching your target audience
195	Your action plan components
196	Own the next step
196	Exercise 10.2: Your action steps
197	Follow through, follow up, level up
197	The value conversation
198	Exercise 10.3: Your value conversation basics
199	Exercise 10.4: More of your value conversation
200	Delivering on the brand promise
201	Finding your systems
202	Exercise 10.5: Finding your systems
202	Start, stop, more and less
202	Strategic neglect
203	Serving clients outside of your target market
203	Exercise 10.6: Self-evaluation and reflection
205	Ongoing validation: Is it working?
205	Results
206	Negative feedback isn't actually negative
207	Exercise 10.7: Create a survey
208	Exercise 10.8: Pinpointing areas for improvement
209	Exercise 10.9: What else?
211	**Appendix**
211	Quiz answers
212	Glossary
216	Acknowledgments
217	About the author

Introduction

Objectives

In every chapter, we'll start by stating clear intentions and goals. I want you to trust the journey you're on and have a clear sense of the value of your final destination — even if you haven't done the work yet to figure out exactly what the right destination is for you.

My intention is for this book to lead you to the best future possible, somewhere you might not even know exists. By the end of this book, you will:

- Uncover what authentically drives you, or more fundamentally, learn how to find it.
- Identify what you want to be known for, by whom, and how you'll deliver it.
- Have a system for putting your brand into motion.
- Understand how to connect more effectively with an audience that needs what you have to offer.
- Be equipped to get "there" faster, wherever "there" is.
- Learn how to evaluate whether your efforts are working to know when to pivot or polish your message.
- Improve how you request and receive feedback, and incorporate it to improve your performance.

Everyone has a personal brand

Like it or not, you have a personal brand — a unique "thing" that clients or customers most strongly associate you with. This could be a first impression, a feeling they have about you or your services, a memorable experience with your product, a personal character trait — even a flaw. It's most likely their observation of what it was like to work with you.

I say "like it or not" because your personal brand isn't always positive. And it's not always a good advertisement that will bring the right kind of customers or work your way. The purpose of this book is to help you guide your personal brand to become one that accelerates your business and attracts more of the right kind of impressions and energy.

For example, would you rather be known as a dreamer, or intuitive problem solver? Would you rather customers choose you because you charge the lowest price, or based on your reputation for being an excellent strategist? These are examples of how personal branding affects your business on a daily basis.

In 35-plus years of coaching and guiding business development, I've developed a way to identify your personal brand, tell your audience what it is and how it can benefit them, and how to do this before they decide for themselves. If you leave it up to other people to decide your brand, it might not be the one you want.

Also, if you're not sure what your brand is — or what direction you want to take it — you might find yourself trying to be everything to everyone. That's a path to mediocrity and probably, misery. And that's also…

Why you need this book

Most personal branding books say you should wear a blue suit, put on a tie, say diplomatic stuff and be a person with a good reputation — punctual, responsible, honest, hardworking, etc.

But that's not true. In my 35 years of business, I've found that these instructions didn't create a personal brand, and have never moved the needle to achieve anyone's business goals.

What's more important than shined shoes and a firm handshake? Crafting an offering that clearly differentiates you from your competitors, and a message that shows why you're the better choice.

You might wonder what that differentiator is. I believe that each of us has something inside of us that comes out over time — no matter what we're doing. We can't help it; it's just our way of being, an approach that comes out in both our business and personal lives.

I'll bet you can think of the person you know who can always make people laugh, even when things are supposed to be serious. Then there's that person who's always trying to make things safer and worrying about risks all the time. Put these two people in the same job and their core traits will eventually surface. They will put their personal, special stamp on each task and use it to benefit their employers or clients.

What do I get when I get you?

What do you uniquely bring to each role or challenge? Don't just say you're "honest," "hardworking," "reliable," or "nice" — see if you can answer it in a way that makes you unique, with qualities that distinguish you from everyone else. Imagine you've just test-driven four cars. What matters isn't what they have in common, but what makes them unique from each other.

Now let's call that something special "It" for now. Most people don't know what their "It" is. Worse, they don't know how or why to value it, or how to communicate it as a benefit to their target audience. When you tell them how much you like their "It-ness," they're likely to dismiss the compliment and say, "Anyone can do that."

But those who recognize what makes their approach special have taken their "It" and made it the centerpiece of their success. It becomes their main purpose in life. And because it gives them an endless source of energy, I call their "It" their atomic energy source. That's why I call it *Atomic Branding*.

I've poured decades of personal coaching advice for businesses into this book. Using the methods I describe here, I have consistently seen people accelerate their careers by years — even decades.

The goal of this workbook is to give you a hands-on guide to create your Atomic Brand, using your unique set of skills, characteristics, experiences, and assets. These are things that people won't find anywhere else — because they're yours and yours alone.

You are one person when you pick up this book, but another when you put it down.

Your Atomic Brand will align with your natural authentic self, your passions, skills, and experiences — allowing you to build trust and loyalty more quickly. And because your Atomic Brand is based on your personality and attributes, exhibiting your brand will come naturally.

As a result, promoting yourself or your business will take less stress and effort. It will help people remember and differentiate you from others in this highly competitive world. Finally, it will also help you to achieve autonomy over your career.

Once you know your brand, you can easily adapt it to any situation or aspect of your life, business or personal. It's highly customizable.

Have you ever found that a particular job caused you a lot of stress? Maybe you could do it, but it wasn't an easy fit for you, or it didn't align with your personal ambitions, so it would take extra energy and stress to get it done. A lot of people struggle with this. They conform to fit a particular job, client, or business, rather than finding the right job or business to fit them.

If you're self-employed, you might find yourself taking on a demanding client who demands additional work out of your normal scope because even though it's not what you want to do, you don't want to refuse the work. In a corporate culture, you might find yourself in the finance department, instead of a creative department, because no one knows your true creative talents or ambitions.

If you're in a marketing department for a company that has a clear brand, you may not like the term "personal brand." That's okay. Use "identity" or "core strength" instead. Remember: in this competitive world, we must differentiate ourselves to stand out and help others choose us — regardless of our situation.

By the end of this book, you'll know your personal Atomic Brand, and how to connect with the right clients and customers to help you achieve success. This book will take you and your business to the next level — whatever that means for you.

Sound lightweight? Unsubstantial? Too soft-skills oriented? Relax and read on. I have an effective, concrete formula that has proven to work consistently and ensure success.

If, at the end of this book, you still don't have the answers you need, feel free to contact me through my website: **CraigRobbinsNextLevel.com**. Likewise, I love reading about your own personal experiences and success stories, so please share those too!

Why me?

You might be thinking, "Why should I choose you?" or, "What's your Atomic Brand? No doubt, your clients ask the same thing about you!"

I gave you a hint in the introduction: I create space for people to go to the next level.

My Atomic Brand is: "I take you to the next level."

I started my career at CBRE, a commercial real estate firm among the Fortune 500, and an S&P 500 company. There, my natural approach and skills led me to uncover details or deals that other investors couldn't find. I became known as the one who found the deals no one else could. In my 15-plus years there, I progressed from sales to senior vice president. I later went on to play key roles in helping two other real estate companies, Colliers International and LoopNet, to grow exponentially, and eventually go public.

Word got out that I was the guy with "next level" skills, and I was headhunted for an exciting new job opportunity. I realized that my unique approach and skills came down to one thing: my natural curiosity. It was my natural curiosity that led me to dig deep and uncover details. I would do a deep dive on a subject to figure it out and then I would help make it better.

So my personal Atomic Brand was born! My curiosity creates space for people and companies to go to the next level.

This Atomic Brand has created a clear differentiation from my competitors, and an awareness of my natural strengths which ultimately led to my success. Today, I'm known as an innovator and next-level thinker. Clients hire me when what they're doing isn't working effectively anymore and they need to find a fresh perspective. They might want this for their business, individual career, customer base, or even product sales.

I've worked with hundreds of companies and individuals over the years, with spectacular results. I've also developed roadmaps and formulas to streamline the process and help people to uncover their true, authentic selves.

My past clients include: General Electric, Coca-Cola, Colliers International executives, City of Hope, Mutual of Omaha, Coldwell Banker, dōTERRA Int., CBRE top teams and producers, Kamehameha Schools, and a wide array of businesses, professionals, managers and top teams. Across all industries, including individuals, small business owners, sales teams, start-ups, and large corporations.

Here are some examples of some unique Atomic Brands I've helped uncover:

- The helpful financial planner: "I make hard decisions easy."
- The marketing specialist whose approach is connecting: "I connect the product to the client's needs."
- The manager who puts things and people together: "I build teams that do extraordinary things."
- The engineer who doesn't like to waste time: "I specialize in delivering optimization."
- The designer who excels at style: "I sit at the desk of cool."
- The chef who loves exploring: "I bring street food to you at a new level."
- The administrative assistant who is always ahead of the game: "I anticipate your needs before you know you have them."
- The beer brewer who is passionate about history: "I brew in the historically authentic German way."

I have hundreds more examples, but you get the idea. I have no doubt that this book can do the same thing for you. You might wonder what your Atomic Brand is, or have an inkling but have never sat down to put it into words. Or maybe you have a clear understanding of how you're different from the rest, but no action plan to share it with the market.

Wherever you are on your journey, I believe this book will help.

How to use this book

This book is a workbook, meant to be scribbled in and dog-eared. As a tool, some sections might feel easier for you, some might be very challenging. That's normal — no one is good at everything. I've also included a glossary at the back of the book for reference.

You might find that over time, as your career goals change, your Atomic Brand needs to be refined. Just flip back to an earlier chapter and work those exercises again with your new knowledge and context. Likewise, you could use this process to develop your own personal brand, and then go back and do it again for your company or business.

I recommend you set aside time to work through the exercises at least a few times a week, or even 15 minutes a day. Your brain is a muscle. The more you flex it, the stronger and better it will work, and the more ingrained these concepts will become.

Reflect on each chapter's objectives before you move on to the next. Go over the exercises. Is there someone else you can join forces with? A friend, accountability buddy or a mentor? Someone you can bounce things off of if you get stuck? By creating two forms of accountability — first on your calendar, and then through a social connection — you're more likely to finish this book and kick off your authentic Atomic Brand.

Before you get started...

Take a few moments to jot down notes on what you want to accomplish with this book. How will you know you're successful? What specifically do you want to improve in your business?

CHAPTER 1:
Why bother with branding?

Objectives

We're easing you into exciting new territory with a big-picture look at the core principles of branding. By the end of this chapter, you will:

- Understand what a brand is — and what it isn't.
- Understand why you need a personal brand.
- Understand how a personal brand is vital to building a successful business.
- Be energized, ambitious, and ready to move forward.

Are you ready? Let's lay the groundwork and go!

The very, very, very first thing to know about branding

Forget what you've been told (and you've probably heard this again and again): Building a successful business depends on building successful relationships.

That's a LIE.

Wait. What?

That's right. It's a lie. Your ability to build your business isn't about relationships at all. It's about branding.

Think about it. A relationship only happens after people decide they want a relationship with you. And they decide that based on their first impressions — what they see or hear from you and about you.

I can take your very best client away.

Don't believe me? I can create almost any relationship I want if I take someone like Tom Brady, Oprah Winfrey or Warren Buffett to a meeting. How? Because a strong brand or identity trumps a personal relationship. A person with a stronger identity can even take away your job if your identity isn't strong or memorable enough. A relationship is a consequence of a strong identity or personal brand.

Think about it. Do you personally know any employees of Coke, Microsoft, Apple, Visa, your 401k retirement plan, your health insurance company, or your electric company? Unlikely. You're probably a longtime customer who has spent thousands of dollars with them — with virtually no personal relationship. Ask yourself: what drives people to work with each other? What precedes a personal relationship, and is, in fact, even stronger? You guessed it. Branding.

We are social creatures. We're wired to interact with each other. That means sharing, exchanging, trading, connecting, and communicating. Our survival depends on it. Without the ability to interact, our lives become impossible (or at least, very difficult).

Imagine falling ill in a remote area where no one can reach you. No matter how much money you have, you won't be able to buy medicine because there's no one to buy medicine from — or bring it to you. Imagine living alone in the desert and not having access to water. How could you offer to help someone build a shady shelter in exchange for water, if there's no one to exchange with?

Being human predisposes us to look for opportunities to exchange with each other because we are more successful at survival when we work with a community. If you cannot transact, you die. If you're not sure about that, watch any Survivor-style reality show. Those who don't transact or have anything to offer their peers get voted off or face mortal peril.

Now let's apply this to branding.

Elon Musk is famous for using "first principles thinking" to keep Tesla at the forefront of electric vehicle innovation. First principles thinking means going back to the beginning — the first principle that holds true — to solve problems. It's the basic assumption that cannot be deduced further. Here are some first principles that apply to branding:

First principles for branding

- Human beings are social creatures.

- Being social enables us to learn from each other, which helps us adapt and survive. Learning from each other is a competitive advantage for our species.

- Learning generally involves an exchange between at least two people.

- People are constantly looking to exchange with each other to increase their chances for survival and quality of life. We share, trade, transact, and exchange all manner of things: physical goods, ideas, help, love, learning, friendship, money, and more. Virtually everything in our lives is traded. Even charity is a trade that makes the giver feel good and hopefully helps the receiver.

- If a person stops transacting with others, they die. Making it easy for people to understand what you have to exchange is critical to your ability to transact. A common language will also accelerate this exchange.

- The more you transact, the greater chance you have to create prosperity. All business is a game where one person is trying to get another person to pay attention to what they're trying to exchange, so they can conduct a transaction and get what they want.

- All businesses have one thing in common: They promise something that will better the quality of life of another person. No matter what your business is, people buy because they believe the product or service will better their lives in some way.

It's not who you know

Many people say, "It's a relationship business. It's not what you know, it's who you know." But, when we understand that personal brand precedes personal relationship, we realize this is not the case.

The people who claim that relationships are the most important thing are often making excuses for why they failed to transact with someone. The first principle is really that a person's brand or identity comes first, then the relationship follows. This is a core principle you will see over and over in this book.

> **Identity** is the interpretation, by self or by others,
> of a person's overall significance.

Here are some practical applications of branding that produces identity preceding a relationship:

- A friendly person in a white shirt and black pants at the front of a restaurant is expected to show you to a table.
- A person who presents a high-prestige credit card or drives a luxury car is expected to be wealthy.
- A person in a uniform with gold wings and a captain's hat is expected to be a pilot.
- A person with a badge and a gun is expected to be in law enforcement.

All of these elements create a first impression and that's a key element in a personal brand.

Appearance is one element of a personal brand that triggers your audience's past experiences, assumptions and expectations. Essentially branding is telling people what they can expect to receive by exchanging with you.

Wait a minute. Does that mean branding is simply a marketing term for stereotyping? Is a brand merely a stereotype in a certain context?

Not exactly. Stereotyping is a part of branding, but it's not all there is to branding. Let's explore this a bit further.

Stereotype vs. brand

If you don't think stereotypes matter, think about it like this: Would you take a random person who smells bad and looks grimy to meet your CEO?

Not likely. Why not? How they present themselves creates an assumption about how they might act — and you are concerned their actions could potentially have a negative effect on your identity.

Perhaps this person is actually a rich angel investor who is too busy to shower or change their clothes. But how would you know that unless you knew them personally for a long time? If you'd only just met this person and that's what they told you, would you believe them? You'd probably want some proof — a testimonial or references from a trusted friend — maybe even a bank statement. That grubby person is going to have to work so much harder to prove they're not what you assume they are. Their brand — what their appearance suggests they have to offer — is pennies in a cup, not millions in the bank.

Likewise, if you take someone neatly dressed in a white shirt and black pants as your guest to a fancy fundraising gala, you can expect that a few people will mistakenly give them drink orders.

Your brand is an expectation of what people will receive if they choose to interact with you. It's your offer to your audience, and how they think you will solve their problems or make them feel.

Whether we like it or not, we stereotype. We judge books by their covers. Our brains process so much visual and audio information that stereotypes are a survival mechanism to help us filter important things about the world around us.

By some estimates, our brains receive up to 11 million bits of information every second at an unconscious level and focus on 40 of them at a conscious level. Stereotyping is largely unconscious, and research shows that the more a person needs to control a situation, the more likely they are to stereotype.

In some situations, a nice suit is what we expect to see at a sales meeting, wedding, or presentation. But would you expect to see your doctor wearing a suit? What about someone working in an art studio or a cafe? In a rock music promoter's office, purple hair and a nose ring are totally appropriate.

All of this points to people making identity observations before they decide if they want to get into a relationship. How you look, what you say, and where you're coming from — your approach — all matter in the first phases of meeting new people.

At an unconscious level, how you look affects your identity. For those who think stereotyping is lazy and arbitrary at best — and biased, discriminatory and prejudiced at worst, I would suggest that because stereotyping is largely unconscious, it will be difficult to overcome assumptions other people make about you.

So at least consider it when meeting with people you wish to transact with. If you ignore how you craft your first impression, it'll take a little more time to change others' initial perception of you. If your appearance doesn't fit with what they're expecting, it could slow or stall your ability to create a clear brand to transact with them.

To be fair, successful relationships help a great deal, but they come after a positive initial assessment — not at the start. That's the big mistake people often make: "Hey, I just want to have a relationship with you for no reason, then maybe down the road we can do business together." No one would be interested in a relationship unless that person had established a personal brand identity up front.

> **""What you are stands over you the while,
> and thunders so that I cannot hear
> what you are saying to the contrary."
> — Emerson**

Now, if Serena Williams or Warren Buffett wanted to form a friendship with you, you might say OK. But imagine if someone called you out of the blue saying, "I'm Jane Smith. I want to be friends with you with the hope of maybe doing business in the future." You'd either hang up or start looking for a catch.

> ### CASE STUDY: From bigwig to nobody
>
> I was given the opportunity to be an extra in a popular sci-fi movie. At the time, I was a global COO of a company with more than 500 offices in 59 countries. Everywhere I went in the business world, I was treated with a high level of attention and respect.
>
> On the movie set, because of the way I dressed and carried myself, actors and workers kept coming up to me, assuming I was in charge. As soon as they discovered I was an extra, their interest evaporated. Some people actually walked away from me while I was mid-sentence. I had nothing to offer them in a movie transaction. As soon as they realized that, I was nothing.
>
> Like many other highly competitive industries, people in entertainment can become hyper focused on the transaction conversation. It's difficult to get people in this mindset to pay attention to things outside of their area of focus. Despite my appearance, I had no real offer or value for them. It was a strange feeling to go from executive to lowest-rung status in seconds.
>
> Can you see the stereotype in action in this example? Just the clothes I wore and the way I carried myself led people to assume I was a producer or director.

Snap judgments

It takes only one-tenth of a second to make a first impression. That's less time than a blink. Studies by clinical psychologists show we draw 11 judgments about someone within seven seconds of meeting them. That's seven seconds to decide if they're going to interact with you.

That gives you just seven seconds to tell someone about who you are. It's vital you use them well. Use them to define yourself with the utmost clarity and set yourself apart from competitors. That's what your brand is.

I once went to Capitol Records for a presentation by a senior executive. He had hair down to the middle of his back, a long beard, a faded t-shirt and jeans — and it totally worked. I'm not saying you should only dress in business attire. I'm saying dress to reflect your brand, because the image you present to your target audience matters.

> ### CASE STUDY: Dress for success
>
> A sleeve of tattoos, a buzz cut, Birkenstocks sandals, or a uniform — these work well in some settings and poorly in others. I was first taught to "dress for success" in one particular way to be accepted. For me (as a man), this required a blue suit, a power tie and no facial hair.
>
> One day, I met the top person in my industry from my biggest competitor. He had long, blond hair, an earring and (gasp!) no tie. Total rock star vibes. He figured out that a lot of institutional people wanted to be wined and dined with the Hollywood crowd, so he promised Hollywood VIP access and insider deals. He used his connections with the Hollywood crowd and took his clients to glamorous and elite places.
>
> This man's brand was the supercool, connected, approachable guy, so he dressed to come across that way. And it worked for him. He excelled at the technical side of the business too. His success, despite breaking the dress-code rules of our industry, made me question what I had been taught. You could say I went back to first principles.

As we go through this book, you will see why dressing like a rock star worked for that person's personal brand strategy. It helped him stand out from a sea of blue suits, in an industry where people can be turned into a commodity.

It's not about what you wear, it's about aligning your appearance with your personal brand. At first glance, this will project an identity and form your first impression. This impression is just one part of building a personal, product, service, or corporate brand.

Presentation is part of your brand, but not the only part. It will help people speed up the process of deciding whether to do business with you. Done right, in a manner that appeals to your audience, you'll be allowed to move to the next stage of a potential transaction. This is the ultimate goal in branding.

Having a strong, clear brand doesn't guarantee they'll choose to transact with you. Maybe you're selling sedans, but they need an SUV. But your brand does differentiate you from your competitors. As a result, when they need you, or if they know someone looking for your products or services, they're much more likely to remember and recommend you.

If you don't have a strong brand, you won't be easily distinguished from your competitors. You risk getting *commoditized*. What does that mean? Read on.

Got commoditized milk?

Let's say you're a local dairy farmer who produces milk. Your potential customers are at the supermarket, staring at a fridge packed full of milk from various brands.

Which milk are they going to buy? What makes them pick the brand they do? Since they can't taste the milk before they buy it, they have to rely on the milk's brand or price (more on pricing later). If a consumer can't distinguish or differentiate you from your competitors, they'll typically make decisions based on price. This is what's called "being commoditized."

When commoditization comes about, the cheapest brand usually wins. The consumer is unable to make their choice based on merit, so they default to "which is the best value?" Without having a personal or emotional connection to the brand, such as growing up with that brand in the house, or personally knowing the farmer (unlikely), price almost always wins.

Commoditization is even more prevalent in the services industry. When you're in competition with other companies for someone's business, but you don't have any personal connection to the potential buyer, you are in a commoditized situation. And if you don't know how to make your services stand out from your competitors, your buyer will likely make a choice based on the cheapest price.

This is why most people say, "Get out there and just network and get to know everybody." When there are loads of competitors and we haven't figured out how to differentiate ourselves, relationships do matter. The flip side is that building these relationships is time consuming and inefficient. It's much easier to have an Atomic Brand.

Back to our milk scenario. Let's slap an organic label on your bottle:

Now you've set yourself apart. You've given your customers a way to differentiate your product from your competitors. You have de-commoditized your milk and taken a stand as organic.

This triggers a value conversation with the customer. It might make them think, "Well, I'm not into organic stuff," or "That fits with my health goals." Either way, creating differentiation with a clear brand identity helps drive the transaction forward, especially when your brand or product reflects a shared personal value. In this case, it might be the idea that "organic" is healthier.

This basic principle of differentiation applies not only to your products or services, but also to your personal approach. Whether you work in a tech company, department store, or roadside fruit stand, your brand helps people see your unique value more clearly.

> **Branding** establishes an instant and lasting emotional connection with your target audience that separates you from your competitors and makes them want to choose you.

It's so instant, it's almost subconscious. And it needs to be, because brains are busy processing and organizing a lot of information. Your potential customer or client won't waste time reading or digging through information to find your hidden value. They want to be told upfront what value you can deliver, so they can make a quick, effortless decision and move on to their next item on the list.

Your strong, effective Atomic Brand will do that for you. It will make it easy for your target audience to distinguish you from your competitors and make a quick decision about transacting with you.

It is reinforced by the first impression you make and how quickly you can make an emotional, memorable connection. This emotional connection is often the product of shared values and goals. Apple didn't just sell computers, it offered tech for creative people. If you consider yourself creative, then you likely have a positive emotional connection with Apple's brand and products.

Conclusion

You've reached the end of Chapter 1, so we've laid the foundation for how to think about branding. By now, you should understand:

- Why it's important to have a strong personal brand.
- The first principles of branding.
- Why your physical image and first impressions are important.
- What commoditization means in business.

CHAPTER 2
What is a brand?

Objectives

Your mission, should you choose to accept it, is to start from a solid foundation of brand knowledge. By the end of this chapter you will:

- Fully understand what a brand is — and isn't.
- Understand the difference between a brand and a logo.
- Learn various ways to differentiate a brand.
- Understand the difference between market position and brand.
- Learn how a brand takes your market position and unique selling points and offers it to your target audience in a way that benefits them.

Our focus in this chapter is establishing how a good brand will help you and your business. Let's roll up our sleeves.

Name that brand

Let's tease your brain with a few fun exercises that illustrate how we perceive brands in our daily lives.

EXERCISE 2.1 Name the company based on its logo

What company do each of these logos belong to?

Write your answers here:

1. _____

2. _____

3. _____

4. _____

5. _____

For correct answers, turn to the "Quiz Answers" section after the conclusion of this book.

EXERCISE 2.2 Name the company based on its tagline

Which brand do each of these slogans or taglines belong to?

1. _____ gives you wings
2. The Ultimate Driving Machine
3. Because you're worth it
4. Overnight
5. Just do it

Write your answers here:

1. _____
2. _____
3. _____
4. _____
5. _____

For correct answers, turn to the "Quiz Answers" section after the conclusion of this book.

What's in a brand?

Is a brand the same as a slogan? Or a symbol? Or logo?

No. Many people get confused by this. They think a brand is just the visual identity of a corporation. While look and feel is important, a logo represents the brand, but it doesn't define it.

In exercise 2.2, I asked you to identify a company based on its slogan. While a slogan reinforces the brand, it isn't the brand itself.

> A **brand** is a promise, from one party to another, about what they can expect to experience from buying a product or service.

The Red Bull slogan, "Red Bull gives you wings," creates the expectation of feeling uplifted and energized after consuming it. This brand is all about the experience created by the product, which we'll go into more detail in the following chapters.

The slogan, "Overnight," creates the expectation that FedEx will deliver your packages fast. When your package is urgent, FedEx most likely comes to your mind. This branding saves you time and energy because you won't need to search for the fastest overnight package delivery service. You already know FedEx is up to the task.

Branding accelerates people's ability to make decisions about buying a product or doing business with each other. This book is designed to help you create a brand conversation about yourself — what experiences you have, what skills you offer, what you're passionate about and what you're disciplined to do.

Next, you'll figure out how to condense this into just a few words. If Orville Redenbacher can find a way to differentiate popcorn, you can do the same for yourself.

When people quickly and easily understand your brand, they can decide whether to work with or buy from you. Your brand builds trust, it tells your customers that they will get a certain level of service or quality.

**Your brand promise can be anything —
positive, neutral, or even negative.**

For example, an ambulance-chasing lawyer might have the reputation for being cheap and ruthless — a "bad" promise. If you don't have a lot of money and are in urgent need of a settlement, they might be exactly what you're looking for.

As another example, basketball player Dennis Rodman was known for his fierce and relentless rebounding abilities, earning him the nickname The Worm. He also got a lot of attention because he looked different, with brightly colored hair and heavy tattoos. He was known as a wild man on the court and off.

Being a nice person in a nice suit — in a sea of other nice people in nice suits — is a recipe for being forgotten. But whether your brand promise is positive or negative, you have to be able to deliver on it.

A promise that you don't deliver on is a failed brand promise. If a moving company promises to carefully wrap, pack and move your entire house without breakage, but then your favorite dish set arrives smashed and your couch is torn, you'll never consider them for your next move. You're also unlikely to recommend them to a friend. Their brand has failed to deliver on its promise.

We'll talk more about how a negative promise can impact personal branding in Chapter 3. And there's another catch: If you don't control your brand, other people will control it for you. This may not be what you want. For some people, the perception of others is as good as it gets. Most people get ignored — they don't even get their brands managed by others.

Elements of a brand

In a nutshell, a strong brand…

- Solves a problem for your target audience.
- Describes how you solve that problem differently.

If you can attach your solution to a higher cause, the brand becomes even more powerful. That's what Tesla did. It offers stylish electric cars that are perceived as a status symbol. But its nobler offer is helping drivers avoid using fossil fuels to save the environment.

Have you ever had an employer or manager describe what you're good at … and it isn't what you think you're good at? It might be because they haven't spent enough time observing what you're good at, or it might be that your approach isn't being recognized the way you'd like it to. This is why you need an Atomic Brand.

I've made a career out of helping people find their brands. Even when my job description focused on running a business, I brought the passion for personal branding with me to share with my employees and colleagues. I push people to identify and share their personal brands because it gives them autonomy and helps to further their careers. As a result, they move forward faster in the direction that they want to go in, and their careers better align with their authentic selves.

Putting it into practice

Once you have a clear Atomic Brand, it becomes much easier to control the narrative — even when you're not in the room. Your brand forms the foundational building blocks for what you'll use to expand your business or career.

Simply stated, the model is:

- Create a clear identity (defining your personal brand)
- Tell it to others
- Do great work
- Ask for referrals
- Measure your results

Note the diagram below. Your personal brand is at the core of your Atomic Brand — but it's not the only element. It's important to know what message you are conveying to your target audience and potential clients. It's equally important to know exactly who they are and if your message is working.

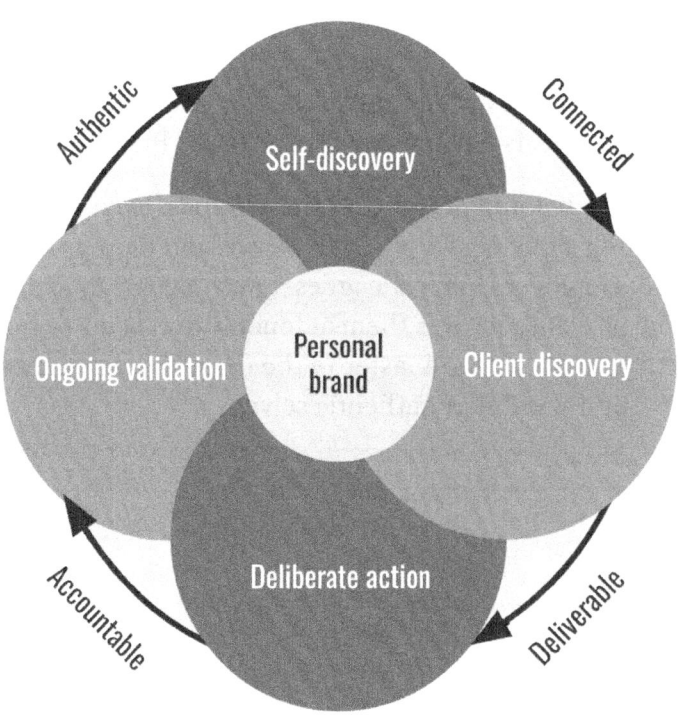

I'll be going into this in much more detail throughout the book. You'll find that being able to define your personal brand is just part of the process. Your brand is meaningless if it doesn't connect with your target audience or help build your client and customer base.

Now we'll look closer at things to consider when defining your Atomic Brand.

DEFINITION: Market Identity

Niche is key. A company positions its products and services based on the beliefs and interests of a specific group of people: their target market.

> **Market identity** is the sum of what you present to your target audience, both visually and verbally.

You can often boil market identity down to a word that embodies what you're going for, then apply it to a target audience. Market identity can be expressed with both visual elements and specific words that make you or your company memorable.

Think of the Nike Swoosh combined with its slogan, "Just do it." Together, these target both serious athletes and people who care about athletic performance. That is Nike's market identity.

Ford brands its F-series trucks as Built Ford Tough. They're "tough" for people who are or want to be seen as having the ability to do tough jobs. Ford even has a commercial where a heavy log drops on a Ford truck in a tough way. If you're trying to portray your service or product as tough, then an F-series truck will subtly reinforce it.

GM, on the other hand, claims to offer "professional-grade" trucks. Its market is professional construction workers, company owners or managers — people who do difficult jobs on a professional level. So their imagery features professionals doing their jobs.

It might not seem like a big deal to you, but these differences really matter to their customer base and that is why they differentiate themselves with market identity. Patagonia promises it makes the best outdoor clothing and protects the planet, eBay offers to "connect people and build communities to create economic opportunity for all," and dōTERRA promises "only 100% pure essential oils."

Your market identity is part of your personal brand. Your market identity includes your physical image, your skills, and your approach all rolled into one. (So far, all we have discussed is your image. We'll get to your skills and approach soon.)

The word "market" sometimes throws people off, but for personal branding it simply means the target group of people you want to know about you. It could be your boss, your coworkers, your clients or your prospects.

Some individual examples or market identity include Warren Buffet, who is known for his approach to "value investing," Gandhi, who is known for "nonviolent resistance," Tom Hanks, known as the "nicest guy in Hollywood," and Madonna, the unapologetic icon who "gets exactly what she wants." Her brand is being a "fully liberated woman."

We will cover all of this in more detail in later chapters.

DEFINITION: Market Position

Circling back to our milk example from Chapter 1, organic milk holds a different market position than ordinary milk. It is considered to be more nutritious, healthier, and antibiotic-free. For a product or company that's long established or has a huge market share, market position can be enough to define its brand.

> **Market position** is how a brand differentiates itself within its sector, compared to its competitors.

Let's look at cola brands. As the original and largest cola brand, Coca-Cola owns the top position in its market. All of its competitors are technically following in Coke's footsteps. It calls itself "The Real Thing" — implying the original is best.

Pepsi differentiates itself by positioning itself not on the product, but on the market that buys Pepsi. It cultivates a younger, edgier brand by appealing to the up-and-coming crowd — the "Pepsi Generation." This positioning implies that being the biggest or oldest isn't always best.

Meanwhile, Red Bull offers you an experience when you drink it — it claims the drink "gives you wings." While Coke offers ordinary moments it calls "the pause that refreshes," Red Bull offers excitement and thrills, embodied in its heavy sponsorship of Formula 1 and daring, extreme sports.

Finally, low-cost private label colas differentiate themselves by offering the lowest price. No flashy ad campaigns, no celebrities, no experiences. Just a six-pack in your fridge for less money than the other brands.

These are four different cola brands with four different market positions. If a fizzy brown beverage can stand out from an entire supermarket aisle's worth of competition, you can too.

But market position isn't the final step. It doesn't differentiate you from other brands that claim the same place in the market. For example, one brand of organic milk holds a different market position from ordinary milk, but it doesn't differentiate itself from other brands of organic milk.

So how can you help your audience choose among brands with a similar market position? Keep reading.

DEFINITION: Approach

This is a key word and concept in Atomic Branding.

> **Approach** is your baseline perspective or point of view. It's the way you bring yourself to a situation, task, interaction or role.

It's a way of being, how you look at something, think about it and act on it. Even if you have no specific skill in something, your approach can still be seen. Do you just figure it out as you go? Do you analyze and research? Do you ask an expert for help?

You'll see the differences in approach in the way someone assembles Ikea furniture. Some will read the directions. Some will methodically unpack everything and ensure they have all the right parts. Some will start assembling things that appear to go together, consulting instructions only when they get stuck. Some will enlist a partner to help.

There are literally a million ways to approach anything. By understanding and articulating your approach, you'll be able to show your target market how your unique approach adds value. In later chapters, we'll dig deeper into finding your unique approach and how to apply it to your Atomic Brand.

You can also think of the approach as how something comes into being. For a product, this is how it gets made. BMW defines its brand as being German engineered. Why? German engineering and assembly are considered by many to be the best in the world. This implies that the product is made with care and precision, and it is articulated with the slogan, "The Ultimate Driving Machine."

For your own Atomic Brand, how you approach a task will further articulate your brand's promise and better set you apart from the competition.

Craft beer is another example. In response to mass-produced, same-old American lager, small-batch microbreweries started to make unique and memorable beers. They approached beer as a passionate exploration, bringing their own style, surprising flavor combinations, and different ways of fermenting malt and hops.

DōTERRA positions its essential oils as the "most pure;" Coors beer extolls the benefits of "mountain spring water" to deliver refreshing, crisp taste; Southwest Airlines offers low-cost tickets with great service, giving normal people the "freedom to move about."

Your unique approach shows up in your unique way of doing things. It's your craft, your product knowledge, your understanding of complex processes and how you relate to your clients' needs. The approach is not just how you deliver your service or product, but also how you improve the lives of the people who use it. Your approach might also involve a unique and specific skill or highly technical knowledge, such as doing surgery, programming, or statistical analysis.

For your own Atomic Brand, how you approach the task to deliver on your brand's promise is a key factor that sets you apart.

CASE STUDY: One job, four approaches

For years, I was a regional manager of a company with more than 10,000 employees. I was personally responsible for 11 offices in seven states. I visited each office and met with every managing director.

I discovered something amazing. Even though each managing director technically had the same job and responsibilities — budgeting, hiring, firing, projections, growth, and more — they all had a completely different approach to fulfilling their duties.

One was very charismatic, keeping the team motivated, happy and energized. Another had excellent attention to detail, so their office was streamlined, with few time-consuming errors. A third was very creative: they were constantly coming up with new ideas, which kept the team mentally engaged. A fourth was a brilliant team-builder, so the office thrived in a supportive and harmonious environment.

Each director used their own innate abilities and unique approach to perform their duties — and each was doing a fantastic job.

DEFINITION: Value Proposition

The value proposition is a promise of consistency. The consumer can expect to receive a product or service of a certain quality, for a certain price, within a specific time frame.

Fast food giant McDonald's is a prime example. It delivers a fast, consistent meal at a very low price. A Big Mac in New York will taste the same as a Big Mac in Moscow, Tokyo, or Johannesburg. Wherever you are in the world, McDonald's promises you a consistent product — in your hands within minutes — at a very low price. In fact, McDonald's is so consistent in their value pricing, that the price of a Big Mac meal is often used as a general economic indicator of a country's cost of living.

The word "value" is a buyer's word, not a seller's word.

Value is what you are producing for them and at what rate, in terms of time and/or money. The buyer — your target audience — gets to decide if what you're offering is of value and worth what you're asking for. You can claim it is all you want, but they get to decide. The added word "proposition" means you are proposing what that value is to your target market and asking them to consider it.

> A **value proposition** is what you are proposing to produce
> for your target market, in terms of time and/or money.

How are you different? How are you better and more able to meet someone else's needs than your competitors? The clearer this value proposition is, the clearer you will stand out from your competitors, and cause the customer, hiring director or boss to choose you.

The word value can be used interchangeably with the terms unique selling point (USP), selling proposition, or brand position. The key is focusing on how it applies to your potential buyer and how you are helping them.

How do you differentiate a brand?

We've discussed some ways you can position a brand within its market. Here are four ways you can further differentiate it from competitors:

DEFINITION: Target Audience or Market

This is a specific group of people you want to use your product or services. It starts with the ideal customer and expands to a larger group who have similar wants and needs. By being selective about the specific target audience for your product, you are describing who would gain the most value from using your products or services.

A new parent is one type of target audience. Another is a business executive. Another is a Dallas Cowboys fan. And let's not forget your boss or potential new employer. Again, the key here is being specific: demographic, firmographic, geographic details, and information on their habits, preferences, values and beliefs can all come into play.

Let's say you're developing a mobile app specifically for Android. Targeting all smartphone users would waste time, energy and resources because some smartphone users won't gain any value from your app. Your target audience is Samsung Galaxy and Google Pixel users, not iPhone users. If your mobile app is a game to help toddlers learn numbers, then your target audience is even more specific: parents of small children who use Android.

So let's say you want to position your boutique brewery as your "area's brewery," and your audience is craft beer people who are proudly from that area and support small businesses. You might name your beer after the area code, like Firestone did for their 805 beer. Similarly, the famous Hatch Valley green chiles from New Mexico were branded with the area code: 505 Southwestern.

I've also seen real estate agents brand themselves for a target market such as Korean buyers by promoting their Korean language skills. On a personal level, if your target is people passionate about preserving marine life, you might want customers to know that you are a professional scuba diver.

DEFINITION: Experience

A brand offers more than just a product or service to its target audience — it offers an emotional encounter. Red Bull promises adventure with the slogan, "Red Bull gives you wings." It also reinforces its experience-based brand by sponsoring a lot of high-octane, high-adrenaline extreme sporting events such as the Red Bull Air Race, snowboarding, cliff-diving and motor cross.

An experience-oriented brand anchors to an emotion that is implied or real when you use it. You might not feel exhilarated when sipping a Red Bull at your office desk, but you're still associating that feeling of extra energy to the experiences Red Bull sponsors. Virtually any brand can be experience-based: a U2 concert is an experience, and so is a shot of tequila.

Disney theme parks do this, so does Ikea. They offer experiences. Dentists do it by adding massage chairs. Tech companies build nap pods, yoga studios and even slides on their campuses. A small business that sells vintage jewelry sets itself apart by exquisitely gift-wrapping every purchase.

But while many companies claim to set themselves apart by delivering the best experience, few actually do.

If you're looking for a new career or looking to level up from your current role, it's important to think about how your personal experience fits in with your target company's branding and corporate culture. You need to set yourself apart by demonstrating how your skills, interests and personal experiences align with what they want to project as a corporate brand.

For example, a travel company that offers deep and detailed travel experiences might only be looking to hire locals that speak multiple languages and grew up in the area. If you want to work at a Disney theme park, you need to be about family fun. Southwest Airlines says the people they like to hire are the social directors for an inclusive, "we like everybody" club.

What experience do you give people?

> ### CASE STUDY: Pancakes at the Waffle House
>
> The Waffle House is a southern restaurant that wants you to feel like you're in a Southern mom's kitchen — with all the antics that come with it.
>
> The first time I went to a Waffle House, I didn't look at the menu and ordered pancakes. The waiter laughed out loud and yelled to the cook, "This guy wants pancakes!" Then he said to me, "This is the Waffle House. We don't do no pancakes here!"
>
> At the end of my meal, he looked me in the eye and said, "You have a super nice day." The experience can be magical, scary, abusive, scary, relaxing, pleasant — you name it.

DEFINITION: Product Position

Many brands differentiate themselves from their competitors by pointing out that they're the biggest, or the best or have the most product or selection. Verizon positions itself as having the best coverage of any cellular network. Google is the biggest search engine and Facebook has the most users on social media. Microsoft owns the top product position for business software, JP Morgan Chase is the biggest bank, and Costco is the leading warehouse club.

This biggest or best claim is a classic positioning strategy, but it's an increasingly difficult way to differentiate your brand — both as a company and a person. In an increasingly competitive market, the biggest and best have lost their impact.

Think about it like this: If someone came to you to buy their product and said, "We are the biggest brand with more than $5 billion in sales," and then someone else said, "We have $4 billion in sales," would it really make that much difference to you?

It might even work against them because you might think a larger business wouldn't give you the attention you want. The car rental company Avis used this underdog positioning to their advantage with a "We try harder" campaign. Their advertising fully admitted that Hertz was bigger, but the implication was that Avis, as the smaller company, would make an effort to provide better service.

On an individual level, many people tell me, "I'm the number one salesperson in the office," or, "I do the most business in this area or specialization." But this type of differentiation can be more confusing.

First of all, people often define best, first or biggest with different measurements, even within the same industry. A restaurant might claim it has the best hamburgers in town, but who decides that? Is this claim based on a local radio station survey, judges at a food fair, or voters from a community newspaper?

Is it important to you to hire the number one dentist, hair stylist, plumber, accountant, painter, massage therapist or personal trainer? Would it really make that much difference if you're happy with the product or service?

On the other hand, if you invented the first index fund, first runners' diet, or a special method or procedure, then feel free to promote yourself as the original. The inventor always has a special slot. But in general, saying you're the top, biggest, largest, most experienced, or most awarded won't matter to your target audience unless they can see how this will benefit them.

Ask yourself: Who owns this position in your industry?

DEFINITION: Pricing

How much your target audience will pay for your product or service can be a high or low price. Walmart and Tiffany's create different expectations of pricing. Price can be driven by quality and availability.

Luxury brands such as Chanel, Louis Vuitton, and Georgio Armani all promise a high-quality product — genuine leather, handmade, exclusive designs — and also create exclusivity by limiting product availability.

Hermés Birkin bags cost from $9,000 per bag and can go for over $100,000 at auction. They are in such high demand, that they've had wait lists of six years. Why? Hermés only produces a limited number each year. Very few people know how many, though some reports suggest under 70,000 per year, which is tiny considering the global reach of the brand. Each bag is considered a piece of art and each maker has to train for more than a decade before they're allowed to make one. Owning one is a statement: "I have arrived."

On the other end of the spectrum, a brand can position itself based on the lowest prices. These are your store-label colas and off-brand products. They might not be as good as the original, but they're close enough to make the substitute worthwhile. This is the value calculation the buyer is making.

In fact, when brands differentiate on price, customers may become suspicious when "extras" are thrown in. Costco promises low prices, so you'd be surprised to see a fancy retail store display in the warehouse. Southwest's brand also promises low prices, so you're going to receive a packet of pretzels and not a full tray of food on your flight.

Pricing applies to people as well.

One lawyer might position herself as the super high-priced attorney with exclusive clientele, while another lawyer offers low-cost services that anyone can afford. I'll bet you can imagine how their offices would look different, and how you would expect to be treated differently in each office as well.

What do you think it costs to have Barack Obama speak at a private event these days? He would absolutely get top-tier pricing. I've often heard from businesses that raised their prices and got more business as a result. In many cases, clients want to know they have the best, and pricing is a signal of quality and status.

After Covid, more and more people have been working from home. Some people have lowered their prices because they like working from home. Some people have raised their prices because they can do their job from anywhere and they are considered the best. Regardless of how you price your services, you need to be able to articulate your value to the customer.

Differentiating your brand or product on low pricing can be tough. Being able to deliver a lower price in a highly competitive market requires an ability to reduce overhead to remain profitable. This often requires huge bargaining power. Large companies like Walmart lower costs by bulk-importing goods made in Vietnam or China, where labor is much cheaper. A boutique supermarket can't compete with Walmart on price — they can't buy in bulk. So they'll need to differentiate based on something else: friendly staff, gourmet selection, or locally sourced produce.

Ask yourself: Where am I on this pricing model?

Most brands combine all four tactics: audience, experience, position and pricing. Take Rolls-Royce. The cars promise a first-class, pampered driving experience: the feeling of gliding along, cushioned in the most perfect, softest leather. The cars are designed for the super wealthy, who expect the best, and the cars are priced accordingly.

Universally, the power of branding is so strong, that you could probably take any industry and instantly identify brands that "own" one of the positioning categories we've discussed.

Try it right now with your local pizza options. Which one is cheapest? Perhaps it's Little Caesar's "pizza pizza," that is, two for the price of one. Which offers a unique experience? Chuck E. Cheese's comes to mind, with the arcade games and kid-centric activities. Which is the first/best position? I'll bet you can think of a local pizza parlor that proudly advertises, "since 1953." And which is for busy parents? Seems like Papa John's "take and bake" offer fits them best.

Let's make branding personal

Differentiation can also be applied to Atomic Branding. We'll go into more detail on this in Chapter 3.

Elon Musk positions himself as a forward thinker, which is reflected in Tesla's commitment to efficiency through better engineering and manufacturing. Musk applies "first principles thinking;" he strips away old ideas and methods that are no longer working to come up with innovative approaches to travel and technology.

Musk's personal brand is cutting-edge efficiency. He is known to question assumptions, ask questions and dig deep, leading to innovation in electric vehicles and space travel to Mars.

Like him or loathe him, self-made rapper Tekashi 6-9 has a personal brand of stirring up controversy, trolling and sparking outrage. He is famous for being infamous. If you've heard of him, you probably know him more by his reputation than his songs. His target audience are people who love to be outspoken, heated, passionate, and assertive. They like their rap in your face, gritty and true to the source. The key word here is audience. That is how Tekashi 6-9 positions himself as different from other rappers.

We can't talk about the power of personal branding without bringing up the Kardashian family. These mega-influencers have built their careers, business ventures and lifestyles on the power of their individual and collective personal brands.

What exactly is Kim Kardashian famous for? Being famous, mostly. But if we dig a little deeper, she's captured a position in the market as a person who knows "how to make yourself look and feel beautiful." She does this by presenting herself as the "most glamorous socialite and businesswoman."

The Kardashians built multi-million-dollar revenue streams on their personal brands, typically in the fashion and beauty categories. Kim epitomizes glamor, wealth, and status, which relate to the pricing and value of her products.

Kim's target audience is women who are willing to spend money to enhance their beauty. Her products and those she endorses reflect this — everything from shoes to diet shakes to shapewear and lighting rings for selfies. While some people dislike her, they're not her target audience, just like not everyone is a fan of Elon Musk. Her brand is positioned on price, with the promise of reassuring luxury.

You can apply the principles of differentiation to people you know or work with. There's the fun person in your office (experience), your house cleaner (price and value), your accountant (target audience) or your oldest friend (first/best).

Before we move on, let's look at something interesting that happens when you create identity. Personal branding means taking a position — and others then decide whether they like or want it. A strong identity can strongly attract one portion of the market, while equally repelling another segment. In fact, there are few people with strong identities who don't have both fans and detractors.

Every president and virtually every prominent athlete, entertainer or actor seems to have their share of haters. Picking a brand creates a position, and that position excludes some portion of the market.

As an example, if you decide your brand is attention to detail, you'll have some people embracing your eagle eye and your ability to dot I's and cross T's. Others might bristle at this identity, saying you're inflexible or can't see the forest for the trees.

This is one big reason a lot of people don't take a position or create a personal brand — it's simply easier to go with the flow. But if you do this, you'll have to subordinate your true self and let the market decide your identity. And that's the road to mediocrity.

So if I've brought up examples of people who you don't admire, don't worry — the point is that their strong identity makes them universally known, not necessarily universally admired.

EXERCISE 2.3 What are these brands known for?

How do these brands differentiate themselves? What are they known for?

1.   FedEx
2.   Farmers Insurance
3.   Chanel

Write your answers here:

1. _____

2. _____

3. _____

For correct answers, turn to the "Quiz Answers" section after the conclusion of this book.

What a brand isn't

By now, you should have a good idea of what a brand is, and how it represents both corporations and people. But there are a lot of things that a brand isn't. Your brand is not just one of these:

- High-quality service
- Personality type
- Years of experience
- Your technical skills (unless they are highly specialized)
- Trustworthiness
- Being a nice person
- Location
- Niche within an industry
- Good value
- Logo (we discussed this already)
- Color scheme or decor
- Tagline or slogan

The descriptions above can be useful in helping you to reinforce your brand, but they're not actually ways to define a brand. While a look and feel is used to express a brand, the brand idea is the promise you're making to the market. You're promising to solve a problem in a unique way, a differentiated approach.

Ask yourself: Could my competitors claim the same things I do? Does my website say things that are also true of my competitors? If the answer is yes, it's time to reevaluate. Focus on the things that make you different — not just being trustworthy or experienced or nice.

Why can't you differentiate on some things?

Why can't you differentiate on attributes like trustworthiness? Because it doesn't make you different.

Everyone says they're trustworthy, experienced, or nice — even criminals. These terms are used so often, they've lost their value. Your competitors will always say they provide quality service. But isn't that an expectation? Isn't being nice a basic requirement for good customer service?

Yes, trustworthiness, price or level of service can be a brand. But in an increasingly competitive and saturated market, it's hard to differentiate yourself unless your brand is already well-established and has considerable market share. These selling points are also so overused that your potential consumers are likely to automatically filter them out and disregard them entirely. Your brand will get lost in the noise.

As an example, virtually every airline claims to be committed to excellent service. We all know that service sometimes falls short, so when choosing an airline, we simply filter this message out.

Southwest Airlines doesn't focus its brand messages on customer service. Yet, out of all of the airlines in America, it consistently ranked among the leaders in customer service. Why don't they spend more time and money advertising these awards? Because that's not the decision driver for their target audience. Instead, Southwest built its brand on low prices, which is a value message that resonates better with customers.

As for longevity, I often hear professionals claim "30 years in the business," as if experience was the best differentiator. But if I used longevity as my criteria for selecting a brand, I would miss out on innovations from Google, Peloton, Uber or Tesla.

Why a slogan isn't a brand

Taglines, slogans, catchphrases and mottoes are ways of reinforcing your brand identity without specifically saying it. "Be all you can be" (U.S. Army recruiting slogan), "It's finger lickin' good" (KFC), "Ideas for life" (Panasonic), and "Think different" (Apple), all say something about what they want you to get from their brand. They all imply a sense of action.

These slogans aren't the brands, but the slogan is intended to create familiarity and drive you to action. Nike's brand may be "Improved athletic performance," but its slogan is "Just do it," — a more concise, friendly and action-oriented phrase.

A memorable line can communicate differentiation and inspire action in a target market. But this slogan must be based on an established brand: the promise to the market to solve a problem differently and better than competitors do.

How do you differentiate from competitors?

It's not what you have, or your point of difference that defines your brand. Unless that difference delivers a selfish benefit to your target audience.

Jeep creates the expectation of feeling like you are ready for a rugged experience. Ritz-Carlton offers you the gold standard experience. Disney gives you a magical experience. Volvo gives you safety.

This is a subtle but important nuance. Volvo doesn't proclaim itself as "safe" — it promises to give you safety. All of these brands focus entirely on their audience's wants and needs.

And companies that make people's lives better are the companies that endure. Like an electric car to cut fossil fuel, a portable computer to give us freedom from the desk, insurance that helps us sleep better at night, or well-thought-out investment advice.

In my life, I watched game consoles evolve from Atari's Pong to the latest interactive Call of Duty. When I started my career, I needed to go downtown to trade stock through a stockbroker. Now I can do that with my phone and an app. The companies that add value to people's lives will make it, and in some cases they will replace other companies or whole industries.

Ask yourself: How are you bettering people's lives?

To build an effective Atomic Brand, you'll focus less on talking about your brand, and focus more on showing your target audience how you can benefit them. Your audience will decide if they value what you offer — you can't make them value it. I'll say it again: value is a buyer's word, not a seller's.

> An **offer** describes how you propose to provide a solution to someone's concern or problem.

Let's go back to our "do not use" terms here. Saying you are the top producer, the largest company, have the most experience, or did the biggest deal, won't matter to your target audience unless you show how it benefits them.

These attributes on their own aren't enough. You need to demonstrate how your attributes solve their problems.

This solution-oriented approach can help differentiate your personal brand. In my years in management, when I interviewed candidates, I'd ask, "Why should I hire you?" Most people replied with some flavor of, "Because I'm loyal, trustworthy and hardworking," or, "I've spent 20 years in this global company," or, "Because I was the top performer in my specialization."

If I printed any of that in an advertisement, it wouldn't mean that much to you. And it didn't mean much to me in an interview. It was forgettable. It was vague. It was roughly what everyone said.

If you go to an interview with a company or prospective client, prepare by figuring out how you're benefiting them. If you can't articulate it, you won't be a good fit.

I found that the minute a candidate said something different that I hadn't heard before, like they loved negotiating, or they were all about taking personal responsibility, then they stood out to me.

> **The idea that your personal brand is based on being trustworthy, the best producer, or most experienced, ignores the methods, skills and approach that got you there.**

That is what people want to hear. Otherwise, your answers are the same as everyone else's. There is only one situation this will work: If you're the only one in the world who does this. As in, you're the only person in the whole world who has the experience, knowledge or skills to make your product or deliver your particular service.

How often will that be the case? And if you truly have that niche capability, your scope will be limited to only performing that one particular task that no one else can do. Once that is completed, there is no reason to continue using your products or services.

Conclusion

The goal of this chapter was to help you learn the ways you can define yourself based on your market position. It's a strong step toward differentiating from your competitors, and you'll take this unique approach and demonstrate how it benefits your target audience.

The Disney brand promise is "to create happiness through magical experiences." The Disney castle logo is not the brand, but it reinforces the idea of a magical experience. Even without the logo, Disney is known for inspiring a sense of magic and wholesome family fun.

But you're not a big company, you're a person.

I'm using a lot of examples of big brands and global companies for ease of recognition and familiarity. But all these principles can be applied to a small local company or a person. After all, Walt Disney was a person who established himself and built a company from there. Same for Jeff Bezos, who started with books and built Amazon to be "the everything store" and for Wolfgang Puck's culinary empire of restaurants and branded foods.

Next time you're out and about, look around at local companies and business owners. Ask yourself: how are they branding themselves? How are they differentiating themselves from their competitors?

By now, you should understand why brand is so important. You've learned how it's different from a market position, and the four elements of market positioning. You're also starting to think about some ways to differentiate your brand from your competitors. You know why it's a bad idea to rely on position or price alone to differentiate your brand. Finally, you've learned that your brand is about taking your market position and points of difference and framing it in a way that benefits your target customer.

Now that you understand the foundational principles of branding, you're well on the way to creating your own brand. So let's go up another level.

Before you move on...

Take a few moments to jot down notes on what you've learned about branding so far. Are there any questions you have, or things that don't make sense? Are you starting to think about how branding can affect your business? What are some specific goals you have for using the power of an Atomic Brand in your business?

CHAPTER 3
Branding a person

Objectives

By the end of this chapter, you will learn:

- The difference between personal and corporate branding.
- Why it's important to have a personal brand (even if you don't know what yours is yet).
- What energizes you and authentically drives you.
- How you connect and follow through with people.
- How you can get "there" faster — wherever "there" is.

Now, let's dig deeper into what a personal brand is.

What is personal branding?

> "At the end of the day people won't remember what you said or did, they will remember how you made them feel."
> — Maya Angelou, author, poet and activist

Let's take what we've established about a brand and look beyond globally recognized companies, products, and services. Let's apply it to people.

Now we're talking about personal branding.

A person's brand is a bit like their reputation. It's how someone is known for the role they play. But a brand is bigger than reputation. Most people don't have an emotional connection to someone else's reputation. Also, a reputation doesn't define someone's values, qualities, or unique approach. But a powerful brand does.

> A **personal brand** is an identity that stimulates a meaningful emotional response in another person about the values and qualities for which you stand.

In other words, a personal brand is the word or phrase you want others to think of when they think of you.

Your personal brand communicates your values, personality, and ability to deliver certain results. It's your personal promise of how you will approach your role and what results you will deliver.

Your personal brand defines your approach and how you do what you do. It's a bit like a stereotype in that it's quick to appear, but leaves a long-lasting impression with other people. Movie actors use it all the time — they call it typecasting. Think of any movies you've seen recently. I'm sure you could easily identify a gangster, diva, mastermind or henchman.

As an example, you walk into a lawyer's office and everyone there is dressed in smart business suits. In this case, the image you see and the stereotype meet up. Your friend told you that the lawyer you're about to meet is a great guy, so you might already assume he's nice or trustworthy. But now you need to see how he practices law differently from other nice or trustworthy lawyers. What does he say to get you to understand how he approaches his practice? That's his brand.

What's the difference between brand and reputation?

People use the word "reputation" as a catchall. "I've got a great person with a good reputation." It's a way of reassuring others that they're trustworthy. When I was growing up, my grandfather used to say the best thing a parent could do for their children is leave them with a good family reputation. To him, the words "good reputation" meant ethical, accountable, and reliable — an assessment by others that you are safe.

But think about it this way: How would you market a reputation? You may quickly realize that it's very limiting and based around all the buzz phrases we try to avoid — "most trusted," "honest," "reliable," etc.

Brand encompasses your reputation to a certain extent. But brand also creates an emotional connection to your audience. Your reputation establishes whether you are safe or not, but that's not enough of a differentiating factor for someone to choose your products or services over another's in a highly competitive industry.

Think of the idea of reputation in terms of cars. While you would likely not choose a car that is unsafe or unreliable, safety and reliability are just minimum standards that most automakers claim. People choose their cars for more reasons — the experience, value, styling, or specific features.

Sports professionals have very strong personal brands. These are defined and nurtured very early on. Their natural skills and passion get recognized, honed and focused. They're trained to "play to their strengths." When they achieve some success, their media presence focuses on their unique approach and how they stand out from other players. Turn on a sports channel and you'll see commentators analyzing their approach in detail. If they're good, their personal brand is handed to them on a silver platter — without the athlete having to do anything but be good at their sport.

Some stand-out people have taken control of their brand and put it in their own words. Wayne Gretzky is known for "skating to where the puck will be;" Muhammad Ali is known to "float like a butterfly, sting like a bee;" and Serena Williams is known as a fearless, relentless powerhouse who has dominated women's tennis for decades. She is an icon for her power — a tough competitor, glamorous, strong, and honest about her competitiveness. She is also fearless in interviews and able to show genuine vulnerability about making mistakes.

Remember, if you don't manage your brand, somebody else will. Sports icons who cultivate their personal brands make them even more powerful.

The same can also be applied to famous celebrities, artists, and performers. Taylor Swift's brand is "All-American," even as she reinvents her image through each new record era. At 16, Madonna said she was going to rule the world on American Bandstand. She never apologized and kept pushing boundaries with her brazen and sometimes controversial music and videos. She paved the way for female artists to explore, claim and exclaim their sexuality without shame. Beyoncé is among the most famous performing artists in the world. Her brand is "fierce" black female empowerment. If you value black female empowerment, then you may connect to her brand in a strong, emotional way.

Kobe Bryant could have said, "I work hard and am honest." Instead, he said he had "mamba mentality" — a relentless desire to win.

> **"Kobe's impact transcends the game of basketball. It transcends life. Mamba mentality is more of an approach than anything else. It's about attacking what's in front of you with passion and purpose, without fear and doubt and without an ounce of quit. No matter what it is, good/bad, success/failure — that's your approach. That's what it means to have mamba mentality. That's what I learned from him."**
> **— New Orleans Saints All-Pro Linebacker Demario Davis**

These celebrities displayed natural talent early on. They also had ambition and passion, which motivated them to achieve greater levels of success. Beyoncé reportedly records all her performances and watches them repeatedly to hone her execution. Quarterback Tom Brady records and studies his opponents' games until he knows their strengths and weaknesses inside and out. He admits he could watch games by himself all day.

True breakout entrepreneurs have found success by pushing past expectations and defining their own personal brands. Richard Branson is known as a risk-taker first, entrepreneur second. His personal brand also sets the tone for the brand of his company, Virgin. Fun and adventurous, but also smart and savvy.

CASE STUDY: Embracing clients' concerns

My father was a very successful attorney — he once won a case in the U.S. Supreme Court. When I asked him what his brand was, he laughed and said he didn't have one. But after thinking about it, he came back to me and said, "I take on all my clients' cases as if they are happening to me." Do you hear his personal branding in that?

Why your personal brand matters

You might be thinking, "I'm not a singer or an athlete. I have a job. What difference does having a personal brand make to me?"

In a corporate world, we don't get singled out often. We don't have talent scouts, critics, talk show hosts and tabloids telling other people why we are different. This is because we're task-oriented, instead of approach-oriented. We don't have people on the sidelines watching our every move.

I've yet to find an office where they celebrate the person who can reconcile a bank account the quickest, or who has the best phone voice. There's no prize for the quickest or best legal brief in a law firm. Just as long as it's accurate and done by the deadline, it's sufficient. And so we just go about our work tasks and hope to eventually get noticed by our superiors, or, failing that, by a recruiter.

With many sports professionals and celebrities, the media tells us what their brand is. This also happens to business leaders. So many people are watching them and talking about how they succeeded, that their brand is established for them. If you asked them, most wouldn't know what their brand was, or it might be a generic reputation-based answer like, "I work hard and I'm honest." But if you asked members of their team, they'd immediately know the leader's brand. They might say, "Jane is super creative," or "Bob is a great strategist." The employees know how Jane and Bob are different from other business leaders due to their unique approach.

In the corporate world, it can be difficult to identify your own personal brand because you're likely thinking of your job description and tasks accomplished, rather than thinking about your unique approach to these responsibilities. But imagine if you did! Imagine how quickly you'd be able to distinguish yourself from colleagues or competitors. You could use this differentiation to build your dream career.

Personal branding in businesses helps you express your authentic self in a way that benefits others. It helps people accelerate decisions about whether to work with you, and why you're the best person for the job.

It also helps you avoid work that's not your strong suit. If person A is known as "unconventional and creative" and person B is known for their "eagle-eye attention to detail," you immediately know which person to bring in for a brainstorming session and which should lead an audit. When you can embrace and articulate your personal brand, more opportunities that are aligned with your best work and passion will show up.

In business, we don't just want your reputation — such as kind, hardworking and trustworthy — to precede you. We also want your community of clients and colleagues to know your approach, unique skill set, and experience, all in a nutshell. As a result, people will know exactly what to expect from you and how you will benefit them. Just like if they bought a bottle of Coca-Cola.

> ### CASE STUDY: Saying no to things outside your offer
>
> Have you ever been selected for something you really didn't want to do, but your boss thought you would be good at it based on your prior work on something (that you also didn't like)?
>
> That happened to me. My boss asked me to run a convention, which is a giant administrative job that I knew I'd be terrible at. It didn't feel like a "next level" assignment for me and I worried I would have delivered less than what he expected for the attendees.
>
> My boss was really surprised when I turned it down, and it took a lot of convincing before I was able to help him understand why it was a bad idea.
>
> I got lucky that time — most of the time, you don't get to say no. If you do say yes (or you don't have a choice), ask your leader if you can do an assignment with your unique approach.
>
> If they say no, it's likely that your offer was not strong enough to convince them, or they don't care and think of you as a tool. It's also possible that you don't have a unique approach, but that should be good motivation to work on it so that you can eventually secure the right job for you.

Your personal brand is pure you

Now we're going to start applying personal brand theory into practical applications. The model below identifies the many aspects that go into making up your personal brand. You'll see how personal branding is the central connector between all the main elements that are going to help you successfully market your business, services, or products.

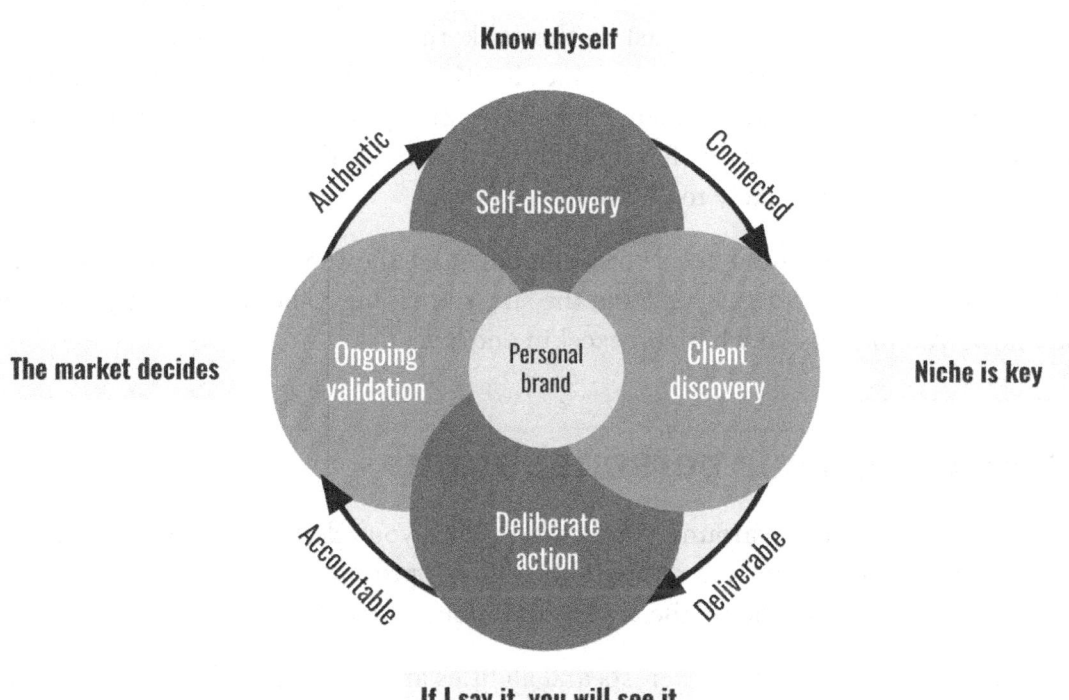

Self-discovery is the key to a successful personal brand, and I'll be taking you through that process in the next chapter. Client discovery is detailed in Chapters 7–10. Deliberate action and ongoing validation are covered in Chapter 11. As you can see, everything fits together. Once you have all the elements in place, you'll have a complete system, which will give you a clear course of action.

Why develop your personal brand? It takes a lot of energy to be someone you're not. Not only is there the everyday stress of your job and duties, but there's the extra energy needed to motivate yourself to do something you dislike and focus on it. If it's something you're passionate about, this isn't an issue.

This is not suggesting that every aspect of your job is going to be thrilling — even doctors must do tedious paperwork. But we want the main aspects of your job to align with what drives you.

You always have a choice. You can design a life where you can be autonomous and self-directed, or you can be subordinated and directed by others. It could even be a mix of both.

People often tell me, "I just want to do my job and not have people bother me." They are under the impression that if they just do the work, they will get the promotions and raises they desire. That might work in some situations — like sports and entertainment — where you have highly aware managers who might spot your potential before you do. However, in a vast majority of cases and particularly in the corporate world, efforts to "just do your job" are likely to go unnoticed.

Taking control of your brand gives you autonomy and allows you to be your authentic self at home and work. It frees you from the stress of trying to be something you're not and allows you to focus on what you excel in and love.

Show them your personal brand

Your job is to teach people around you — whether it's your clients, colleagues, or employer — why your personal offer, capabilities, and approach is better than others. Teach them how having you on the team will uniquely benefit them.

If you really think your skills, interests and abilities aren't being fully utilized by your employer, then you have a duty to tell them. If you know you'd be happier and more effective in a different department, then staying where you are not only impacts your happiness, but it also impacts your productivity, the people around you, and the company.

Likewise, if you're self-employed, you have a responsibility to communicate to your potential clients why your services are better, because this benefits them.

It's a competitive, crowded, busy, information-saturated world out there, and it takes some work to differentiate yourself. But I promise, it's worth it.

A good personal brand helps you stand out from the pack.

Let's say you work in a corporate office. The person who handles expense accounts gets angry when there's a mistake on the expense form or a missing receipt. Their brand is sharp and ruthless. They are known to miss nothing and come after you if you do. They probably don't realize it, but many of the account executives dread submitting expense forms. They have been given a brand by their work colleagues, that they're not even aware of, and they have no control over it.

Let's stay with this example for a moment and dig a little deeper. Perhaps this account expense person works in an advertising agency. Maybe they're good at their job because they have razor-sharp analytical skills, so they've been employed to police the sometimes-sloppy sales team.

What they'd actually like to do is use their amazing skills to analyze advertising spends, and get clients the best return for their advertising dollars. Instead, they've been pigeonholed into accounts, become known for it, and got stuck there.

Subordinating your own personal identity for the sake of the company gets you pigeonholed and makes you miserable.

When people get stuck like this, their personal brand is not in sync with their authentic self and motivations. They often must leave the company for a different job. Or if they stay, they become increasingly miserable — counting years, months, and days until their retirement.

No wonder our account expense handler is so unpleasant. They're probably very unhappy but afraid to ask for more.

According to the U.S. Bureau of Labor Statistics, Millennials (people born between 1981 and 1996) hold an average of 8.2 jobs between ages 18 and 32. However, Baby Boomers (people born between 1946 and 1964) held 12.3 jobs from ages 18 to 52 years old, according to a National Longitudinal Survey from the U.S. Department of Labor.

That means that a Boomer's average tenure at work is more than 2.75 years per job, while a Millennial's average tenure is only a little over a year and half.

When I do personal branding work, I find it's the older generation that tend to get their brand faster. Why? They've had more jobs where they've had a chance to use it — and for it to be effective.

Many Boomers found that they used it once and got a promotion. But in their new role, their personal brand wasn't valued, so they had mixed results. They either got laid off, moved on, or they simply adopted a new approach to suit the role (rather than finding the role to suit their brand). Sure, they ended up in a job with more money, but they weren't a natural fit and became miserable while trying to fit in.

By having a strongly developed personal brand, you avoid this battle. You'll be savvy enough to assess a promotion and see if it's a good fit for you. If it's a dead end, you might not take it. Or, having a good understanding of how you operate, you might be able to negotiate a position to better suit you.

> **CASE STUDY: What if a promotion isn't a good fit?**
>
> At one time in my career, my boss recommended me for a promotion. The new position was a detail-oriented role with a goal of keeping the company on an even keel. In short, it wasn't a next-level opportunity, and it required a skill set I knew I wouldn't be able to deliver.
>
> So I turned it down because I knew I would melt down trying to fit a role that didn't fit me. It was counter to my brand of "delivering the next level." Looking back, I'm glad I turned it down because better opportunities came my way. Consider your promotions carefully. If the new position doesn't fit with your brand and ambitions, is it worth it?

Your personal brand doesn't have to be nice

Simon Cowell's brand on American Idol is harshly critical. Mike Tyson's a terrifying, formidable opponent. Sam Zell, billionaire and founder of the Equity Investments Group, was known as a tough negotiator. He even had a nickname, "The Grave Dancer." This goes back to the 1970s, where he attributed his success to dancing on the skeletons of other people's mistakes.

Fearsome as these personal brands are, there's no doubt they leave us with a powerful and long-lasting impression, without us even meeting them personally. They're not likable, but they are definitely formidable and respected in their chosen arenas. While Cowell's brutal delivery can be unkind, American Idol contestants still value his feedback; in fact, they need it. Do you want a nice, likable attorney, or do you want someone tough who can get you the best deal?

You can be successful, known and respected for being a ruthless hard ass, if that's what your target market wants and if that's authentic and true to yourself. Cowell, Tyson, and Zell are all examples of authentic personal brands. That's what also makes them so effective. We believe Mike Tyson is intimidating because he really is ... but the market can also spot fakers from miles away.

Your personal brand doesn't have to be job-specific

Imagine if instead of trying to retain the Empire's tight grip on the galaxy, Darth Vader had channeled his manipulation and tough negotiating skills into law school. He'd have made a formidable lawyer. One you'd wish you could afford to hire if you needed someone to help you fight a legal battle. Would it still be true to his brand? Absolutely.

We're taught that personal brands should reflect higher virtues: diligence, reliability, politeness, honesty. But that's not necessarily true. For a personal brand to be effective and make you memorable, it needs to be authentic and evoke a strong, emotional response. If it's not true to you, it becomes too difficult to maintain, causes stress and makes you miserable.

> ### CASE STUDY: A negative brand can work, too
>
> One of my clients, Jack, was a top producer in the commercial real estate brokerage leasing industry. He was looking to branch out into real estate investments, but had difficulty attracting the high-profile clients he wanted.
>
> Why? He was whip-smart, impatient, and said what he thought. In other words, sometimes he was abrasive. Yes, he was diligent, hard-working and honest — but those were not the traits he was known for.
>
> After working with me, Jack realized that his strong personality meant he was a hard (almost brutal) negotiator. So he re-branded himself as such. The first client who hired Jack was putting together a complicated business deal with Sam Zell himself. They needed someone who could hold their own against Sam. They hired Jack for that very reason.
>
> In the end, Jack's brand as a tough negotiator stuck and helped him to climb to the top of his company.

Choosing your personal brand

I'm sure in our case study, Jack was a hard negotiator as a kid — whether it was negotiating baseball card swaps or curfew times with his parents. He had that energy and drive from the get-go. He was able to make a successful career out of that energy and identity because it was a natural extension of his authentic self.

Similarly, Bruce Springsteen made a career out of being a blue-collar American. That was who he was from birth, and it's reflected in his music. People that like his music relates to the everyday life struggles he sings about.

Limiting our brand gives us unlimited possibilities. My clients have sometimes struggled with defining their personal brands because they're afraid that by narrowing down a brand, they're limiting their options. They are afraid they won't appeal to people who prefer things that aren't part of the brand.

The reality is the exact opposite. A focused personal brand actually delivers more and better resonance with your desired audience. Take Jack — he's known as a brutal negotiator. Does that mean he's not diligent or honest? No. His honesty is what makes him so abrasive — he doesn't dance around the truth. An actor concerned about being typecast might turn down yet another gangster role, but as a result misses a pivotal role in which a bad gangster becomes a father and tries to turn his life around.

By choosing our brand, we actually expand our opportunities. People who choose usually go further and develop more prosperity and more career satisfaction. They have found out who they are, and they've maximized this to their greatest advantage. This allows them to reject work that's not the right fit for them without fear. They then find other opportunities open to them that are a better fit with their authentic selves.

> **CASE STUDY: From bookkeeper to creative writer**
>
> I worked with a creative writer who was supplementing her income by bookkeeping. The problem was, she hated bookkeeping. As a result, she constantly put it off, did it at the last minute and made small errors that caused irritation with her clients.
>
> She was scared to pursue her writing full-time because she was worried she wasn't good enough, but she constantly found the writing work she was getting was suffering, because she had to put it aside for bookkeeping.
>
> After working with me, she realized her approach was, "helping other people find their voice." Her personal brand was helping people who couldn't — or didn't have time — to write, put their ideas on the page. She let go of the bookkeeping and focused on helping clients get their writing done. She hasn't been out of work since.

Why your passion for 1980s punk rock matters

Let's dig a bit deeper with personal branding. The movies you like, the music you listen to, the experiences you cultivate — it all matters. The foods you eat and even the stores you shop at matter.

Humans exchange with each other on many levels: products, services, friendship, affection, ideas, learning, work, beliefs, and on and on. The faster they understand our identities, the faster they can decide whether to exchange with us.

A punk musician trying to increase their record sales is unlikely to find a new audience at a classical symphony orchestra concert. Their personal brand expression — think leather, spikes, and punk-styled hair — isn't going to resonate with these concertgoers.

Finding your personal brand not only helps you become more confident, feel happier and grow as a person, but it also helps other people around you. It allows you to quickly decide who you need to engage with to grow your business, which makes it easier for you to reach out to them, and easier for them to find you.

The point of branding is to convey the message about who you are, as succinctly as possible. And ideally this message precedes your first interaction with them.

Sounds like a lot? Don't panic. In the next few chapters, I'm going to show you how to build your personal brand from the ground up.

EXERCISE 3.1: Other people's brands

Think about the following people. What are they best known for? What is their brand? You can list more than one of each if you feel like it.
Jot down your responses.

1. Your CEO or someone you used to work for

2. A colleague, someone in your office, or someone you worked with

3. Someone in an organization you belong to

4. Someone in your group of friends

5. A family member

6. Someone who inspires you

As an example, a CEO I used to work for was known for his winning strategies. He would listen to everyone's ideas on how to win, and then come up with another idea on the spur of the moment. The idea would be so good, but also so obvious, that everyone would be amazed they didn't think of it themselves. It happened so often that people started saying, "Let's start with your idea and just do that, you always have a better strategy."

EXERCISE 3.2: First impressions

Jot down some quick answers to these — two or three words maximum. Remember — personal branding is all about first impressions, so don't overthink it. **What do you think the following people would say about you?**

1. People in your industry

   _____

2. In your office/workplace

   _____

3. In the organizations you belong to — you can list each one, or pick one

   _____

4. Your group of friends

   _____

5. Your family members

   _____

6. Your best friend

   _____

EXERCISE 3.3: Are you consistent?

Now have a look at the list from exercise 3.2. **Which answers best describe how you think you really are?**

_____

_____

_____

How consistent is the list? Would they all say the same thing about you, or do you think people from different areas in your life would describe you differently?

Often, people tell me they're a different person at work than at home. When they go to their place of business, they put on a hat and take on a role. This might be viewed as multi-faceted — but really, it's inauthentic. They're not being true to themselves.

People think they have to adapt or pretend to be good at something, because in their minds, there is no other choice. Eventually, they forget they are pretending. They think at some point in the future they will be able to be themselves. So, they assume the role given to them and slog on, miserable.

Unfortunately, we are taught that this is normal. At school, we are taught how to fit in, rather than to define ourselves and find a path in life that fits us. A lot of very talented people were miserable in school because they didn't fit in. A lot of them are successful now because they've found their own path after finishing school. Others who never defined their own paths may just be punching a clock, waiting for retirement, or hoping to win the lottery so they can quit a miserable job.

The higher you move up the corporate ladder, the more you find people who think of themselves as the same at work and home. Good CEOs appear naturally good at what they do because they're able to be the same person all the time. Tony Robbins's wife, Sage, describes him as the same person at home and on the stage. Richard Branson is just as energetic and curious in person as he is in the office.

If you're one of those people who is very different at work, then you're reading the right book. My aim is to help you find your authentic personal brand and use that to find the job or connect with clients who value your brand. This authenticity is actually a recipe for happiness, at home and at work.

> ### CASE STUDY: Using your passion to find your purpose
>
> John Grisham was a criminal trial lawyer in a small Southern town. He loved to connect with people through church, baseball, or the library. He also had a burning desire to write novels.
>
> So he wrote late into the evenings after he finished court. His Southern upbringing, criminal law background, and witness to injustice and racial issues gave his writing a unique voice and perspective.
>
> His second book, *The Firm*, became a massive bestseller. His passions, work and attributes all led to the formation of his brand — gripping crime stories that explore injustice. Now he's a full-time crime writer and has published more than 40 bestsellers.

What's not your personal brand?

"Be yourself. Everybody else is taken."
— Oscar Wilde

As I mentioned earlier, none of the following make up your personal brand. They're so overused that they're not compelling, and rarely create any differentiation. In short, they're commoditized.

- Years of experience in your job or field
- Your expertise (more on this later)
- Your geographic area or where you do business.
- Your product or service type ("I'm a tax accountant" or "I sell life insurance")
- Your company
- You are honest, trustworthy, or hardworking

Words like honest, hardworking, trustworthy, experienced, knowledgeable, best, top, or your job title and job description should not be used to describe your brand. It's like describing milk as "white, liquid and nourishing." Of course it is. If it can't effectively be a differentiator, it shouldn't be part of a brand.

You might ask, "Why doesn't being the top salesperson differentiate me?" You've learned that these are simply market positions — a reflection of where you stand in your industry. They don't speak to your unique approach or why someone should choose you over a competitor.

Most people default to "I have many years of experience" to suggest their competence, or "I am very honest and professional" to suggest their sincerity. Again, these are not personal brands. These are merely attempting to build trust by demonstrating a level of competence or sincerity.

As I've mentioned before, these are basic standards for safety and hold little value with your target audience. It's also a lazy way to distinguish a brand because everyone's doing it. You're going to be different! You're going to stand out for being your own person with an awesome, unique approach.

For example, a person who is really well connected could use this as a differentiator for winning new clients, or in a nonprofit setting could target celebrities and high-net-worth individuals for fundraising. Their hook could be, "I connect you to the right people."

Something else you should know about your personal brand

I have a bit of bad news here. Right now, you are who the market says you are. Whatever you think your personal brand is at the moment, is likely not what others think it is.

Have you ever had a friend who thinks they're funny, but they're not? Go to their friends and ask — they know she's not funny. What a person thinks about themselves is not necessarily what the market thinks about them.

So, for now, you are who the market says you are. Your target audience, clients, and customers already have an opinion of your value. They own your brand. The mission of this book is to help you own your brand, and through deliberate work you can craft and share it. That's the goal of an authentic, Atomic Brand.

If you don't own your brand, it will own you.

Imagine you have one person in your office who's known for being level-headed and giving great advice. Then you ask them what their brand is, and they say either they don't have one, or say something generic like, "I've always tried to be honest and hardworking. My clients trust me." But you know their real brand is that they give great, counterintuitive advice. The problem is they're not even aware of it, so they don't own it and aren't controlling the message — the rest of your office does.

After 10 or 15 years of doing something, most people have developed a brand: a specific skill set, knowledge, and unique approach. But they often have trouble describing it to other people. If this applies to you, you don't own your brand — it owns you.

However, successful people narrow their focus and get really good at it. Then they leverage this into areas where they want to create prosperity in. Often, they do this unconsciously. People who know their brand have higher earnings, more business growth, better job prospects and more career clarity. They are also rewarded with an authentic role that has less stress, takes less effort, and produces greater career satisfaction.

You can have this too. You can take ownership of your brand. And you can start now.

You can change how the market views you

In six months, you can change how the market sees you. If your brand right now is simply what the market thinks you are, or if the market doesn't think of you at all, you have the potential to define and share an Atomic Brand.

> *"There is only one thing worse than being talked about, and that is not being talked about."*
> — Oscar Wilde

There's a parable about a group of blind men who are asked to describe an elephant, something they have never before encountered. Each person describes the elephant differently based on the small piece of evidence they can touch and feel: it's like a tree trunk, a wall, a fan, a rope, or a spear.

This is what happens when people remember you: they believe one interaction is representative of your whole brand. The problem? What if the part they first see doesn't align with your passions, abilities, or goals? You're a whole elephant, not just a tree trunk. So your goal in branding is for someone to see, through a small interaction with you, the brand that's part of the whole you.

> **CASE STUDY: Keep pressing for the right opportunity**
>
> I was a financial analyst at the start of my career and I was good at it. The trouble was, I wanted to go into the sales side of my business. But I had a hard time convincing my managers I could do it because all they saw was my strength in financial analysis.
>
> First, I pestered the managers. When that didn't work, I found a senior producer who needed help in analysis, and I convinced him I could sell my analysis. Eventually, they gave me a chance in sales. After that, I made Rookie of the Year among a bunch of other really good rookies.

EXERCISE 3.4: Brevity is key

Describe your best-friend (or close friend) to someone else — out loud.

Examples:

- Funny
- Loyal
- Thoughtful
- Caring

How many words did you use to describe them? I'm assuming not many. Maybe four or five at most? If you're only using four words to describe your best friend, what are the odds a casual acquaintance or colleague will give you more than four?

Your market (people who don't know you at all) is only going to give you about two words. At best. And that is at best, because it's likely they won't think about you at all.

If you don't tell the market what to think about you, the market's not going to think about you.

Unless you did something so huge, so spectacular that they have to take notice. Even then, people forget. We all know who the first man on the moon was, and maybe even the second, but what about the third? Do you remember who that was?

Your actions have to back up what you're telling people to think about you. This will make you memorable. This is very easy in sports and entertainment, but not so easy in the real world. How do you do it within a corporation or as someone who is self-employed?

Start by finding out what the market is saying about you, and compare this to what you want them to say about you. What's the common link between them? Ask yourself: **Who's your market? Who do you want to know you?**

Make it snappy

If you don't have a succinct way to describe yourself to your potential audience, you're dead in the water. Your personal brand needs to be both unique and clear. Boil it down until it sticks in peoples' brains. For example, if I say, "cool technology," you might say, "Apple."

Having a clear message builds strong brand equity, because it helps the market remember what you stand for.

> **Brand equity** is the residual emotional experience someone takes away from an interaction with you.

In other words, you want your brand equity to be so strong, you're not only remembered by someone, but they also tell someone else about you. Good brand equity means you have a good share of your client's memory when they think of your space. That's called "mindshare."

Ideally, your Atomic Brand takes up a prime spot in your target audience or client's brain. Consider this question:

What's the word or phrase you want others to think of when they think of you?

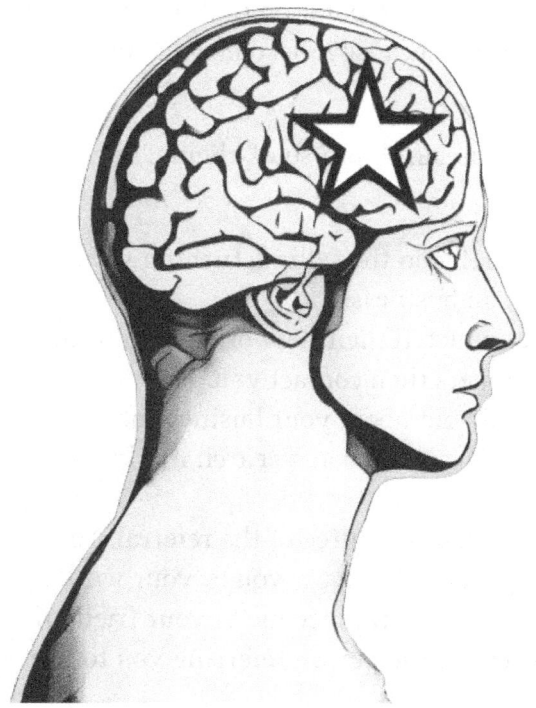

Brand equity is driven by elements such as loyalty, awareness, quality, perceived value, association, and preferences. We need to simplify this to a succinct emotional thought about you. It must be easily remembered and easy to communicate to others.

In order for your brand to introduce what you're about even before you meet someone, your message must be:

- **Authentic** — if it's not a true reflection of you, it won't be easy to maintain
- **Easy to identify** — people immediately perceive it
- **Strong** — it evokes an emotional connection
- **Narrow** — being specific makes it easier to remember
- **Consistent** — so it's credible and expected
- **Connected** — it matches your audience's needs — makes them want to remember you
- **Memorable** — it evokes strong emotions so that it embeds in their memory

Why brand matters to potential clients and customers

Having a clear message makes it easier for people to grasp your brand more quickly. They'll instantly understand what you have to offer that's better than the competition. This will go a long way in building a reputation that precedes you. A clear message also makes marketing yourself easier because it becomes the main theme or message that you'll build on.

A good personal brand will help build "pre-sold" clients. In general, there are three ways to acquire new clients:

- **Direct sales** — you personally do the selling, turning strangers into clients by making a compelling offer to do business.
- **Referrals** — people you know tell their network (who are strangers to you) about your business; these strangers then contact you.
- **Marketing** — strangers find out about your business offer through various channels (such as advertising, PR, social media and search marketing); they then contact you.

Referrals rely on trust in the original source of the referral. You're pre-sold, but your pool is much smaller — it's people who know you or your work personally. Referrals show that you are safe. Would you introduce me to your friend if you didn't know I was safe? Safety is the first concern of the person referring you to someone else.

The last thing I would want is to get a phone call from a friend I'd referred someone to, and my friend says, "Craig, why did you send that guy to me? He's an idiot!" To get referrals, ensure your identity includes safety for their relationship between the person referring and the person who they are putting you in front of.

Marketing is a more effective way to be pre-sold because it doesn't require you to reach out directly to people. When you have a strong personal brand and a clear message, potential clients will instantly know what you have to offer them — even if they don't know you personally.

You'll know your personal branding is working when two people in a room are saying the same thing about you as it relates to your brand.

Key elements of your personal brand

I'll go into this in more detail, but in a nutshell, these are some of the crucial elements of your personal brand:

- Technical expertise (skill, craft, professional ability, practice, etc.)
- Your unique approach
- Your target clients and their needs
- An offer to your clients or customers

> ### CASE STUDY: Using a natural approach to benefit the client
>
> Technically, I was good at real estate investing. My approach was that I was naturally curious. I liked to dig in and find stuff other people couldn't.
>
> A lot of my clients were having trouble finding the right investment opportunities. So I told them I would help them find opportunities they couldn't on their own.
>
> Here is where I used my first two brand elements ("curiosity" and "digging") to address my clients' needs and make offers to them.

EXERCISE 3.5: Your big billboard

Here's one way to help you find your message. Imagine you buy a big billboard to tell people who you are and what you have to offer them. You put it on the biggest, busiest road for everyone to see. What does it say?

Ask yourself: **What's the benefit to the person receiving your services? What do people get when they work with you?**

Mine says: "How to go to the next level in your business."

Try creating a billboard for yourself. What do they get when they get you?

Conclusion

Your personal brand is the foundation on which all of your marketing strategies will be built. Referring back again to this diagram below, your self-discovery is just part of the picture when it comes to creating your Atomic Brand.

Without the other elements (client discovery, deliberate action and ongoing validation), it's meaningless. In the next few chapters, we'll delve into self-discovery and beyond.

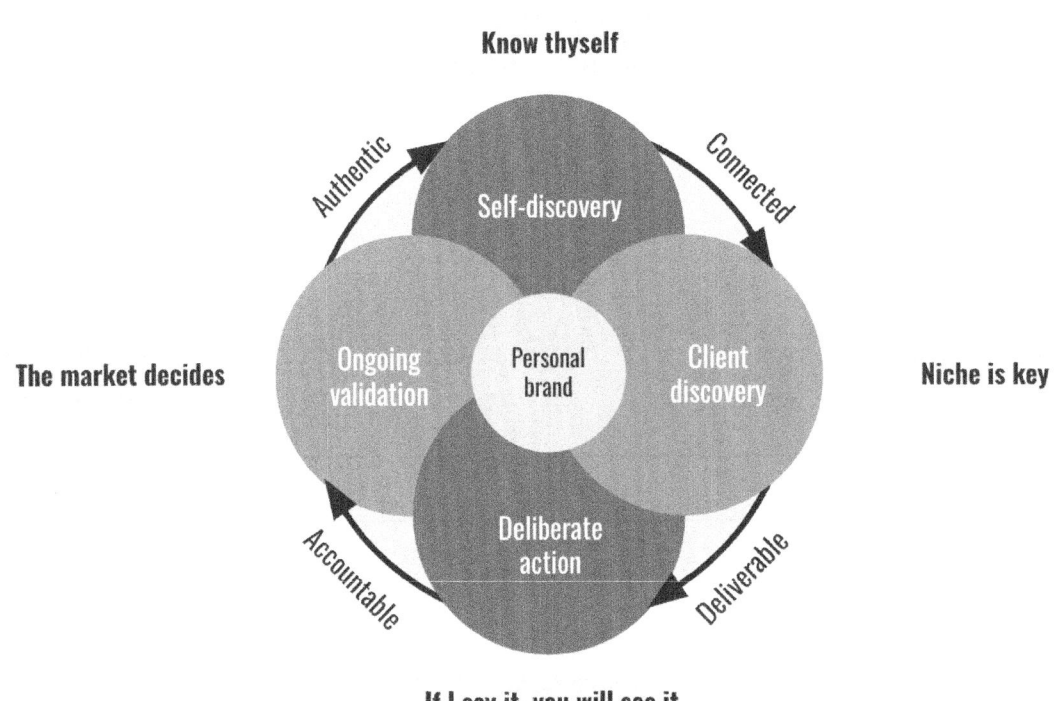

CHAPTER 4
Generating your personal brand

Objectives

Now that you have a firm grasp of the core principles of branding, I'm going to take you through a system to generate your own brand.

By the end of this chapter, you will be able to answer this basic question: What do you want to be known for?

That's it — for now. But it's more involved than it initially seems. It's vital to get this right, because this becomes the core for all of your personal branding.

Eventually this will lead to these questions:

- Who do you want to know about your personal brand?
- How are you going to deliver it?
- How will you know if it's working?

These questions will lead you to find your ideal target audience in the following chapters. But for now, let's discover what you want to be known for.

Control it, or it controls you

> "I can be a better me than anyone can."
> — Diana Ross

There's a difference between having a personal brand and generating it. As we mentioned in the last chapter, many people have a personal brand. They just don't know what it is.

We've talked about how people around you already have a set of expectations and assessments about interacting with you. If you're not telling them what your brand is, they will create their own assessment, and it's not necessarily what you want.

An effective personal brand will help your target audience remember you more easily. This increases the chances of them telling other people about you ... and more importantly, saying what you want them to say. As a result, you're successfully directing the conversation and getting other people to promote you — without you being there.

Now let's focus on our main chapter objective: What do you want to be known for? We'll answer this question through a process of self-discovery.

> "Know thyself."
> — Socrates

Self-discovery is at the core of your personal brand. This is where the real work begins! Up until now, it's been theory. But now, you're going to apply it to your life. In this chapter, we'll focus on discovering your unique approach.

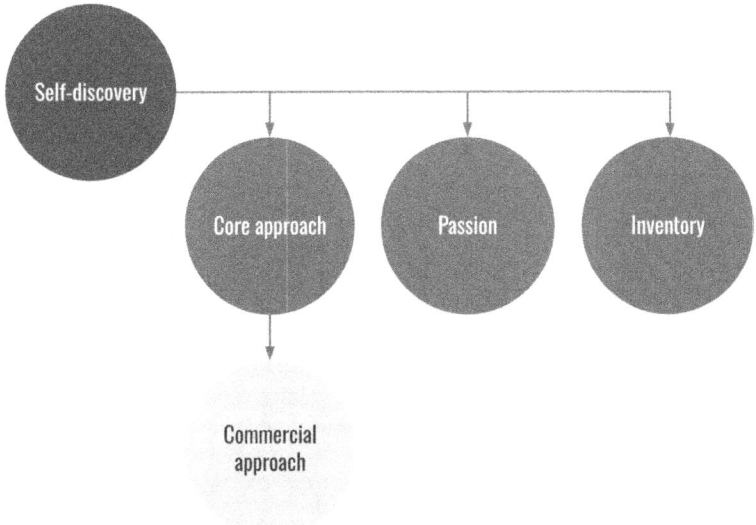

It's a common existential crisis. Who are you really? At your very core? If you're not really sure, that's okay. Lots of people aren't. Plus, as we grow, our goals and dreams, even our likes and dislikes, change. I used to hate brussels sprouts as a kid. Now they're one of my favorite side dishes.

We're going to focus on who you are, right now. Remember: Self-discovery is only part of personal branding. We'll still need to take what your authentic core is and apply it to the needs of your potential client, so it's a clear value proposition for them.

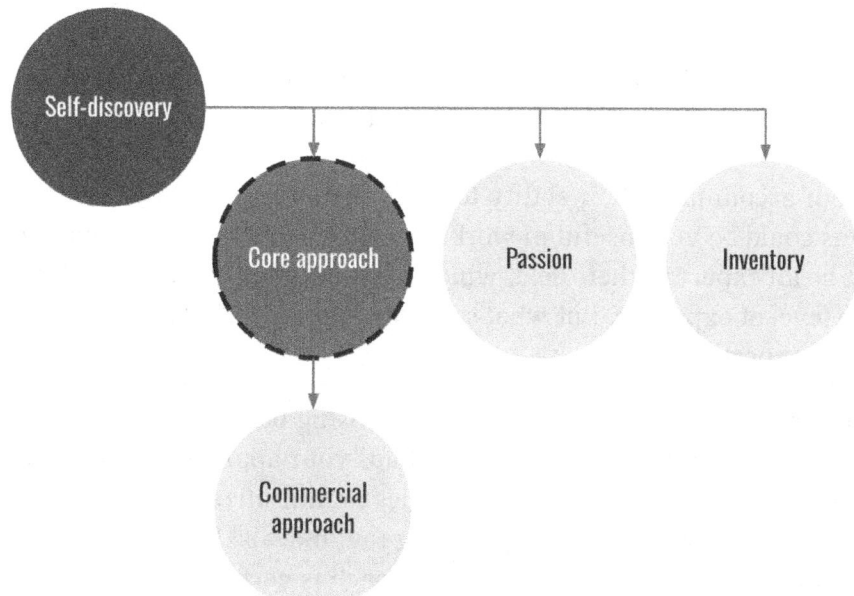

A lot of people define themselves by what they do — their concept of self is based on how they make money, like a doctor, plumber or dressmaker.

That might be effective in a small community where only one person does each of those jobs and can make enough money doing it. However, we're increasingly in a global market. Not only do you face numerous competitors in your own town or city, but you also face them online and across global markets. You are more than just your job, and your job description is not unique enough to separate you from your competitors.

Bringing up the milk example from Chapter 1, there's more than one brand of organic milk these days. And if you consider the number of brands that are now interstate, national, or owned by international companies, differentiation becomes even more difficult, so a brand must be more specific.

If you've defined yourself only by your job or role, this won't transfer very well when you decide to change jobs — particularly if you want to move to a different industry or function. If someone working in an accounting department wanted to move into client relations, on the surface this wouldn't translate very well. You wouldn't expect someone good at financial analysis and spreadsheets to necessarily be good with people.

However, if you focus instead on the how of what you do — not the what — you'll reveal your unique approach. And this can translate perfectly between roles, companies, or industries.

Approach is the way you naturally bring yourself to a task, an interaction or role.

So, back to our accountant: their ability to analyze numbers and figures to solve financial problems could be very useful in working with clients who have financial issues. They might be an expert in their field, which is great because clients will typically want a high level of expertise. But what's important here is to get specific and define why you're an expert.

If you are a corporate attorney and a client is choosing between two expert corporate attorneys — why would they choose you? Perhaps your approach is to focus on risk avoidance and develop comprehensive strategies to minimize risk. Or perhaps you're extremely vigilant and excellent at negotiating tough deals. Both require a technical expertise that is close to the other, but the approach is very different.

CASE STUDY: Partners with different strengths

The most successful U.S. investor, Warren Buffet, is known as the deal maker who looks for value. His partner, Charlie Munger, is known as the risk assessor, who balances the team. Buffet understands how his unique approach benefits his clients and ensures it's complemented by Munger's, who is more cautious and takes a more risk-managed approach.

> ### CASE STUDY: Using a personal brand for career growth
>
> One of my colleagues in commercial real estate did all sorts of marketing activities, from communications to video production, website copywriting, social media, and brand design. Although she worked for the same company for eight years, she held four very different roles in the marketing organization.
>
> Across all of her various marketing activities, she was known as a "firestarter" who could kick off projects quickly, brainstorm in torrents, and move forward fast without a lot of direction and debate.
>
> That's what helped her move up within the organization: execs saw her personal brand and wanted her "firestarter" approach to accelerate their own projects.
>
> When she decided to change industries and move into tech, a competitive field where hiring managers prefer tech experience, she used her personal brand of being a "firestarter" to convince startups that she could quickly build marketing functions from scratch and accelerate their growth.
>
> Now she has worked for seven tech startups (again, in various marketing disciplines) to multiply the revenue of these companies by 5x, 10x or more.

Finding your approach can also reveal your underlying belief system. In the case study about Warren Buffet, you see his belief that "there is value to be found," while Charlie Munger believes "there is risk in all things."

And in the case study above, you see the firestarter has an optimistic belief in the excitement and promise of new things. She sees her job as getting more people excited about them.

As you think about your approach, consider what this approach reveals about what you believe to be true about the world and about yourself. Some might call this a "world view."

Key elements of your approach

Let's dig deeper into your approach. You will most likely find that it's been there throughout your life — from childhood to high school to your career. It's effortless and comes naturally to you, so in most cases, you undervalue it. Take a moment to observe how your approach shows up in your life:

- **Consistency** means that your approach shows up in all areas of your life. Are you a list person? Do you have a timetable — even for when you're working from home or doing an extracurricular activity? Do you let paperwork build up or file it straight away? Do you allot blocks of time to complete certain tasks?

- **Observable** means that others can see your approach in action. People might walk past your office and see your whiteboard, ask you to add things to your list, put things in your pile for filing, or ask for your help in prioritizing tasks.

- **Habitual** means that your approach is so ingrained, you might not even be aware you're doing it. One client I worked with had the habit of finishing every conversation by re-capping and clarifying next steps. When she would talk to her mom on the phone, she'd end the conversation by promising to figure out dates for the next visit or send a new recipe. She did it in work meetings, too: summarizing decisions and speaking to a clear course of action so every person knew who was responsible for which task.

My client didn't think of her summarizing habit as her unique approach. She just wanted to make sure she hadn't missed anything and hadn't dropped the ball. What she didn't realize was that her habit was incredibly valuable, ensuring her team had clear communication and everyone understood deadlines and requirements. What a great approach!

When faced with something new or something you're interested in, what do you naturally do out of habit?

The following section is an exercise to help get the ball rolling for you. Don't worry if you don't identify with any (or just one) category. There's more than one way to find your approach. In the next section, there are alternative exercises and methods to help you. So, pick whichever path works best, or do them all just for kicks.

Pretend you're going to a restaurant with some friends — one you've never been to before. All you've heard is that it's supposed to have a really good menu. How would you approach going to the restaurant, meeting your friends, ordering food and eating there?

How do you approach your role?

Before we talk about different types of approaches, let's review what approach means again. This is the single most important definition, in my opinion, for this whole book:

Approach is the way you naturally bring yourself to a task, an interaction or role.

Now let's consider four different work styles that broadly define how different people approach their roles. As you read the definitions, weigh whether that seems to fit you, or perhaps you'll identify it as the hallmark of one of your colleagues.

DEFINITION: Thinkers

Thinkers tend to operate by logic, data, structure, precision, and method. A thinker is the person who wants no surprises and needs to know the menu in advance — before they even leave for the restaurant. They often want to control where they sit and they might ask for special things from the waiter. They have already thought about how they want things to be.

> Key phrases: Strategy, certainty, figures out angles, master planner, wants rational backup, in charge, directing, out-thinking, declarative, logical, wisdom.

DEFINITION: Analyzers

Analyzers read the menu cover to cover and really assess their choices. They often have not only looked up the restaurant beforehand but have read the reviews and can tell you what the most popular dish is.

> Key phrases: Analytical, research, investigate, audit, evaluate, cost-benefit focus, looks for deals, risk manager, securitized, safety, deliberate, prudent, thorough, exacting, standards, assessment.

DEFINITION: Do-ers

Do-ers are the people who get it done. They are considered people in motion who would rather tackle a task themselves than sit in a meeting. In restaurants, they're the people who get the reservation, make sure everyone is coming, arrange the seating and get checks split. They don't waste time studying the menu and will make a quick decision. At a Super Bowl party, they're the first to get up at a break and head to the kitchen for more chips for everybody without being asked.

> Key phrases: Have to do today, busy, helpful, involved, together, accomplished, competitive, challenge-oriented, stability, reliability, structure, action, sincerity, inclusive, productive, alliance, justice, builder, agreeable, diligent, dependable, consistent, "YES" people, can-do, connected, insider, gossip.

DEFINITION: Intuits

Intuits tend to rely on their instincts, intuition and gut responses. They don't look up restaurants beforehand, they choose their meal based on what they feel like at the time. They've checked the vibe, and they're likely setting the mood for the group.

> Key phrases: Creative, influencer, mood builder, enjoyable, fearless, action oriented, makes it fun, inspires, relates, connects, out-of-the-box thinking, empathetic, get it going, networker, moving, fast-paced, enthusiastic, life of the party, entertainer.

You might notice that none of the key phrases above are functional or technical roles like social media, financial analyst or logistics. That's because this isn't about your skill set, it's all about your dominant approach.

EXERCISE 4.1 What's your dominant approach?

Which of the above would you say is your most typical or dominant approach? You might ask yourself this question in another way: Which style do I default to? Which one is my natural way of operating? Which would my partner or close colleagues say is most me?

Rank them in order:

_____

_____

_____

_____

If you don't really see yourself as any of these, don't panic. Just keep reading. On the following pages I'll share an alternative method for your self-discovery.

EXERCISE 4.2 Make it an action

Now let's take your first and most dominant approach (thinker, analyzer, do-er or intuit) and make it into an action — that's what I like to call a combination of "a verb with an adjective."

For example, let's say the approach that fits you best is "thinker." Think is your action word — a verb. So, let's add an adjective, such as one of these:

- Deep thinker
- Creative thinker
- Logical thinker
- Out-thinker
- Holistic thinker
- Efficient thinker
- Philosophical thinker
- Defensive thinker
- Wisest thinker
- Out-of-the box thinker
- Rational thinker
- Analytical thinker

What would yours be? Write it down. Remember: There's no right or wrong answer. Have fun and let yourself play.

_____

_____

_____

_____

EXERCISE 4.3: Discovering your action phrase

Now that you have your adjective and verb combination, have some fun and turn it into your action phrase. Here are some examples:

- I will out-think or outsmart the competition
- I'll be an innovative or creative thinker
- I'll offer out-of-the box thinking, looking beyond my industry or specialization
- I'll think differently than my competitor or customer does about problems
- I'll think like a business owner, being deeply invested
- I'll think three moves ahead to win strategically
- I'll dive deep in research to understand all the options
- I'll be your think tank partner, willing to play devil's advocate
- I'll think of more equitable solutions to benefit everyone with a winning strategy

What can you come up with?

_____

_____

_____

_____

Again, if these exercises don't help you define your approach, that's okay. We're now going to explore other methods to help you. When diving into these exercises, it's important that you don't just say what you think you should be, but rather what you are. The real you approach is the one people will remember you by.

If you feel like you've nailed this portion of the workbook, you can skip ahead to "The missing words" section later in this chapter. Otherwise, keep going and we'll work on some alternative exercises to help you dig deeper.

ALTERNATIVE EXERCISE 4.4: Building your glossary

Circle at least 20 words from below that best describe your habitual approach. Try to pick at least 20. Add some words if you need to (but not commodity words!). These are words that best describe who you really are — not who you want to be or where you want to work. The goal is to uncover where your strengths lie, and then play them up.

As you highlight the words that best describe you, you might draw connections between them for their similarities, their uniqueness from other people with a similar offer, or their ability to capture attention.

Accepting	Caring	Controlling
Accessible	Certain	Cooperative
Accomplished	Challenging	Coordinating
Accountable	Change-oriented	Correct
Accurate	Charismatic	Courageous
Action-oriented	Charming	Courteous
Active	Cheerful	Crafty
Adaptable	Classy	Creative
Adventurous	Clean	Credible
Aggressive	Clear	Critical
Agile	Clear-Minded	Critical thinking
Ambitious	Clever	Cunning
Amiable	Collaborative	Curious
Analytic	Comforting	Daring
Anticipatory	Committed	Decisive
Appreciative	Communicative	Dedicated
Approachable	Community-minded	Delegating
Assertive	Compassionate	Democratic
Attentive	Competent	Dependable
Available	Competitive	Detail-oriented
Balanced	Composed	Determined
Bold	Comprehensive	Different
Brave	Confident	Dignified
Brilliant	Confrontational	Diligent
Calm	Connected	Diplomatic
Candid	Connecting	Direct
Capable	Conscientious	Directing
Careful	Consistent	Discerning

Disciplined	Fierce	Informal
Discreet	Firm	Informative
Dominant	Flexible	Innovative
Down-to-earth	Fluent	Inquisitive
Driven	Future-facing	Insightful
Driving	Forgiving	Inspirational
Durable	Formal	Inspired
Dutiful	Formidable	Intelligence
Eager	Freewheeling	Intensity
Economical	Free-Thinking	International
Educated	Fresh	Intuitive
Effective	Friendly	Inventive
Efficient	Frugal	Investigatory
Elegant	Fun	Inviting
Empathic	Generous	Irreverent
Empowering	Genius	Joyful
Encouraging	Genuine	Lasting
Energetic	Global	Leading
Engaged	Gracious	Learning
Entertaining	Grateful	Level-Headed
Enthusiastic	Great	Listening
Entrepreneurial	Growth-oriented	Lively
Equitable	Guiding	Local
Essential	Happy	Logical
Evaluating	Harmonious	Malleable
Exceed Expectations	Healthy	Mature
Excited	Helpful	Meaningful
Exciting	Heroic	Meek
Exhilarating	Hopeful	Mellow
Experienced	Hospitable	Memorable
Expert	Humorous	Meticulous
Exploratory	Imaginative	Mindful
Expressive	Immovable	Moderate
Extroverted	Impactful	Modest
Exuberant	Impartial	Motivated
Famous	Improving	Motivating
Fast	Independent	Neat
Fearless	Individual	Neighborly
Ferocious	Industrious	Nimble

No-nonsense
Non-conforming
Nurturing
Obedient
Objective
Open
Open-minded
Opinionated
Opportunistic
Optimistic
Orderly
Organized
Original
Outrageous
Outspoken
Partnering
Passionate
Patient
Peaceful
People-oriented
Perceptive
Perfectionist
Persistent
Personable
Persuasive
Planning
Playful
Pleasant
Poised
Polished
Polite
Popular
Positive
Potent
Powerful
Practical
Pragmatic
Precise
Prepared

Preservational
Proud
Private
Proactive
Productive
Professional
Progressive
Prosperous
Prudent
Punctual
Quality-driven
Rational
Real
Realistic
Reasonable
Refined
Reflective
Relationship-oriented
Relaxed
Reliable
Researching
Resilient
Resolute
Resourceful
Respectful
Responsible
Responsive
Restrained
Results-oriented
Reverent
Rigorous
Risk Taking
Rule-bound
Rule-enforcing
Safe
Secure
Self-aware
Self-motivated
Self-controlled

Self-directed
Selfless
Self-reliant
Sensitive
Serene
Serious
Service-oriented
Sharing
Shrewd
Silly
Simplifying
Sincere
Skillful
Smart
Social
Solid
Speedy
Spontaneous
Stable
Standardizing
Stealth
Strategic
Strong
Structured
Studious
Sturdy
Successful
Supportive
Sustainable
Sympathetic
Synergistic
Systematizing
Take-charge
Talented
Team building
Team-oriented
Temperate
Thankful
Thorough

Thoughtful	Unique	Winning
Timely	Useful	Wise
Tireless	Valiant	Witty
Tolerant	Vigorous	Wondering
Tough	Visionary	Work/life-balanced
Traditional	Vivacious	Worldwide
Tranquil	Warm	Yes-minded
Transparent	Watchful	Youthful
Understanding	Welcoming	Zen
Unflappable	Willful	Zesty

Now, **compile the best of the words** above to better describe who you are and how you approach customers, clients or any situation:

_____   _____

_____   _____

_____   _____

_____   _____

_____   _____

_____   _____

_____   _____

_____   _____

_____   _____

_____   _____

ALTERNATIVE EXERCISE 4.5: Finding your theme

Take your 20 words and group them in ways that fit together. For example, "driven" might fit with "self-motivated" and "persistent." See if there's a better word that summarizes the group, or pick the most representative word for the group. You might even pick the word in that group that is most unusual (but most you).

Think of these groups of words as themes. You might notice you have more words in some groups than others. You might have only two or three word groups. That's fine. This is all a directional exercise to reveal where your strengths are.

Group 1:

Theme:

Group 2:

Theme:

Group 3:

Theme:

Group 4:

Theme:

ALTERNATIVE EXERCISE 4.6: Narrowing it down

Now you're going to narrow it down even further. Look at your words and groups of words.

Select the top five words (or the top group) that best describe your strengths:

_____   _____

_____   _____

_____

Ask yourself: Would these top 5 strengths be confirmed by your:

- Co-workers?
- Family?
- Close friends?

Reflect on how you feel about the energy contained in these words. Do they make you feel energy up, neutral or down? Which of these feel effortless to you? These are likely to be your main strengths, as they have always been important and easy for you.

_____

_____

_____

_____

_____

_____

_____

Now we're getting to what makes you tick. Your way — your unique approach. This is also your authentic self — your truth. It's pure you.

Now we're going to take these strengths or action phrases that drive and distinguish you and we're going to level up. We're going to frame them in a way that makes them appealing to your desired audience.

Why? Your personal brand is in the eye of the beholder — your potential clients, customers, coworkers and bosses decide if your brand is beneficial to them. We need to take your core approach — your natural strengths — and make your clients see the benefits.

The missing words

When you consider the descriptive words in exercise 4.4, do you notice anything missing? (Hint: I've mentioned these previously). The missing words include:

- Honest
- Hardworking
- Trustworthy
- Experienced
- Knowledgeable
- Best
- Top agent, top salesperson, top whatever
- A trade skill or job title, such as dentist, lawyer, broker, programmer, hair stylist (these words are what you do, not your approach, which is how you do it)
- Tech-savvy, social media-savvy

Why aren't these words listed? Because they're commodity words — they're so overused, they've lost all meaning. You'll want to avoid them at all costs because they do nothing to make your brand memorable or differentiate you. Why? If you're any good at your job, it's already assumed that you have these attributes.

People assume when they book a hotel room that they'll get a bed and bathroom. They assume when they buy a car that the tires come with it. Likewise, they assume when they hire you that you (or anyone else claiming to be a professional in your field) that they'll get someone who is experienced and trustworthy. Those are table stakes.

Differentiation only happens when you can offer someone something they don't assume they'll get from everyone else.

There are some jobs that also imply a type of approach, such as scientist, researcher or analyst. This issue comes up when a demographic researcher might be trying to differentiate themselves from others. In this case, they still have to identify their unique approach to their professional work and ask themselves, what do they do differently from all other demographic researchers?

> "Your time is limited, so don't waste it living someone else's life. Don't be trapped by dogma — which is living with the results of other people's thinking. Don't let the noise of other's opinions drown out your own inner voice. And most importantly, have the courage to follow your heart and intuition. They somehow already know what you truly want to become. Everything else is secondary."
> — Steve Jobs

Your approach must be relevant to your client's current needs. Think about words that were used all the time in the past to show a competitive advantage but are now obsolete, such as: ABS brakes, tech-savvy, Microsoft Office-capable, or fast typing speed. Now, every car has ABS brakes, and it's assumed that everyone is somewhat tech-savvy — or at least knows how to use MS Office. These have become basic expectations of many office jobs and are therefore not a point of differentiation.

Consider the expectations of your trade and your customers' basic expectations. All of your competitors likely offer these basics too, so you can't differentiate between them.

If you're finding that your unique approach isn't so unique, or it's in danger of becoming obsolete, then it's crucial to pivot and rebrand yourself, or you'll simply get lost in the noise.

CASE STUDY: Fuji vs. Kodak

Kodak was the main brand for cameras and film production in the USA from the 1930s. Its motto, "A Kodak moment," is still a part of everyday lexicon. Fujifilm was a competitor: a Japanese company that distinguished itself on price.

When digital cameras came into the market, Kodak was slow to adapt. Even though it produced one of the first self-contained digital cameras, it was slow to bring out newer models and keep up. It relied on its branding, expecting sentimentality and customer loyalty. But it failed to recognize the evolving digital needs of its customer base.

As a result, Fuji moved in as leader of the digital market and ultimately Kodak filed for bankruptcy in 2009. Fuji also adapted its technology of film processing into radiology and biotechnology. Today, it is a company known for being in the forefront of medical research and development.

Now that we've covered some of the "don'ts," let's dive into the "dos"!

EXERCISE 4.7 "I'm your go-to person for ..."

Complete the following sentence based on what you've just discovered. Choose what fits you best, then we'll take it a step further and refine it for your target audience.

I'm your go-to person for...

_____

_____

_____

_____

_____

Some ways you might finish this sentence are: Helping you out-think your competition; getting the best deal; deeply understanding your problems; finding surprising connections; anticipating and moving fastest; getting the most bang for your buck; willing to buck convention; able to find allies and support systems; getting an improbable project off the ground; finding the best-fit team to make things happen; turning over rocks to find things other people don't; willingness to do a "dirty job" with a smile.

What's in it for me?

People who consider using your services will ask, "What's in it for me?" (WIIFM) They're not listening for your unique approach, they're listening for how that approach serves their needs. Put another way, your brand is in the eye of the beholder. It's how you want to be seen and remembered by your target audience.

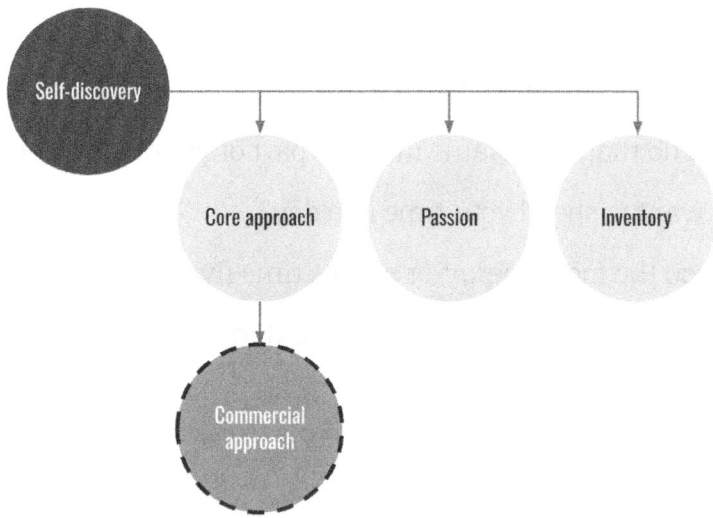

That means we need to refine how you describe your core approach so your audience can see clearly how it benefits them. We're going to convert your features into the client's benefit.

This makes your unique approach commercially viable, and now your commercial approach will drive people to choose you instead of your competitors.

EXERCISE 4.8: Make yourself commercial

How does your approach benefit your target audience of potential clients or customers?

You might start with a lot of ideas — that's okay. Keep digging and then we'll narrow it down. It's easier to work with too much than too little. Again, this is a process — so I've given you lots of space to do it.

If you're having trouble seeing the commercial benefit of your action phrase/strengths from previous exercises, here are some jumping off points that might spark something:

- How do you live and manage your life? What are your strengths?
- What are you an expert at, or becoming an expert at? This could be your skills, craft, technical expertise.
- What do you want to be known for in business?
- If you summed up yourself in one or a few words, what would it/they be?
- What is it you do that is the same in every part of your job, history, and life?
- How do you want to spend your time in a day?
- What gives you the most energy, or makes time fly when you're doing it?
- How can you take your descriptive words and make them something a client would pay for?
- Do people compliment you on a job well done using the same descriptions of how you uniquely delivered?
- Are there certain things you do that others admire, but that feel innate and obvious to you?
- Consider the inverse of your career: where would your unique approach be utterly wasted? In a job with tons of structure, a job that doesn't require much creativity, or a job that's more about efficiency than finesse?

Jot down some ideas about how your strengths or action phrases would help someone.

CASE STUDY: My self-discovery exercise

My five action words were: relationship-oriented, curious, efficient, creative and competitive.

CORE APPROACH	COMMERCIAL APPROACH
Relationship-oriented	→ Connect to the right people
Curious	→ Next level
I don't waste time	→ Efficiency
Creative	→ Effective
Competitive	→ Winning strategies

When I thought about how those would benefit my potential clients, I realized that one of my key drivers was my curiosity. I love to dig deep, explore new ideas and research options.

After being in real estate for 15 years, I wanted to make a change. From doing these exercises, I knew my unique approach was my curiosity and competitive nature. I needed a position that would use my natural curiosity to deliver results.

But that wasn't going to fly on its own — why would they care if I'm curious? I needed to demonstrate how my curiosity, competitive nature and ability to connect with people would be a positive or desirable consequence to my future employer. So, I came up with this: I specialize in getting you to the Next Level.

When I met with the CEO of Colliers International, I told him that I used systems, technology and people to do that. He said, "That's exactly what I want this department to do, and I want to be the first one to go to the next level."

That was a great defining moment for me. I was hired and never looked back. Finally, my career path was aligned with my authentic, personal Atomic Brand.

Your commercial approach is easily adaptable. Your how can apply to each new what in your career: future jobs, a new industry, or a different clientele. It's easy to tailor — without you having to change who you are to do it, because while your job may change, how you approach it remains constant.

That's a win-win! You stay authentic to yourself, work within your natural approach and abilities, and your clients benefit from it. But don't start sending out job applications (or marketing emails) yet ... we're still on this journey of self-discovery.

> **CASE STUDY: A brand without a reason to transact**
>
> A friend of mine was an artist and decided his brand was that "he wasn't commercial." Basically, he was saying he didn't want to transact with other people and didn't want to sell his art or make money. He called that being a sellout. He was very poor and never sold any of his work — which was a shame, because he was very talented.

Your brand needs to be something your target audience wants and can transact with. And there's an audience for nearly anything, including people (or art) that is confrontational, nonconforming or shocking. Your brand can embrace an edgy approach, so long as your market sees value in it.

EXERCISE 4.9: For the sake of ...

When you make something commercial, you want the market to understand why you're doing it. Consider how people view politicians — they see the good ones as "selfless public servants" or "champions of a cause," and the bad ones as "self-serving career politicians" or "they just crave power."

If people don't understand a positive motivation behind your commercial offer, they're very likely to assume it's negative. If you propose to build a corporate department or function, some might assume you're trying to gain power or grab more of the budget. But if you show them that you want to build a corporate function for the sake of improving things for the business or employees, more people will align with your offer.

For example, when I started Colliers University, the corporate training division within the global commercial real estate company Colliers International, many divisions and leaders around the world thought I was trying to grab their training budget. The real reason I wanted to build Colliers University was because I wanted junior brokers to receive the best training in the world, so that we could build the next generation. Only when the divisional leaders understood my reason were they willing to back this ambitious new project.

Let's uncover why you're making a commercial offer. Keep digging into your answers above by asking, "For the sake of what do you deliver? Why do what you do?" Your answer reveals what drives you, and why you care about the work you do.

If your first answers are "for the sake of me making money," "for the sake of being No. 1" or "I just want to be happy," then dig deeper. You might get to "I feel accomplishment and self-worth when I finish X" or "I'm building a legacy for X."

Your answer to why you do what you do ultimately needs to connect to a purpose beyond yourself: it could be for the sake of others, for the sake of a problem that needs solving, a system that needs fixing, or a situation that needs attention, like a cause or a movement.

In fact, making money or achieving success in your career is simply a consequence of first building a strong identity and then pairing it with the necessary skills to deliver on your promise.

I like to ask people, "How would you describe what you do as if it is a cause or movement?" As a real estate broker, I realized what I did was balance out an unfair information situation, so both buyer and seller could feel good about the transaction. The market needs a balance of information to accelerate the ability to decide. That was my cause.

So what's yours? You do this for the sake of what? Remember: Dig deep!

For the sake of _____ , I do _____

For the sake of _____ , I do _____

For the sake of _____ , I do _____

For the sake of _____ , I do _____

For the sake of _____ , I do _____

Some people use their current job as an excuse for not generating a personal brand. But companies and markets change, so it doesn't make sense to get comfortable in one job and expect you'll never be called on to make a change.

Besides, this journey of self-discovery has very little to do with your current job. It's about identifying your natural attributes and authentic desires, and shaping your career around them. If you ignore them, you're at risk of being pigeon-holed.

Personal branding can be an extra challenge if you're currently operating "out of position," meaning your current role demands you function outside of your authentic brand. You may be pretending to be something you're not, like a creative type in a compliance-heavy job, or a strategic thinker in a procedure-driven role. Even if you're playing out of position, you still have a personal brand. But right now, you're not able to align your role to your brand.

If you continue accepting a role that doesn't fit the personal brand you intend, you could forget what you thought was the "authentic you" in the first place. If you ignore it long enough, you're in danger of becoming a clock-watcher — counting the days, hours, and seconds until retirement. You'll be toiling away at the daily grind and becoming increasingly resentful of people who come to work smiling and saying they love their jobs.

I see that a lot. I see people suffering because they never gave themselves permission to explore their authentic selves, or put in the work and took the risks toward creating a fulfilling, autonomous career. They collect wages, pack their true selves away from 9 to 5 (what I call "subordinating their identity"), and call it a job. But it's never, ever a calling.

This is your chance for change! Embrace it. You'll be amazed at where it can take you.

While you're on the path to a personally fulfilling professional life, don't imagine it will be 100% fun. No matter the occupation, everyone does chores. Things that suck, but still need to be done. You won't be able to use your approach as an excuse not to do what needs to be done.

For example, a doctor might love consulting with patients and hate entering data and notes, but they still have to do that for every consultation. They can't rely on their memories. A writer might love creative writing but hate proofreading. They'll need to self-edit or hire a proofreader, or an embarrassing typo might go on display for the world to see.

No job is without its have-tos. Ignoring them could be detrimental to your current and future positions. Negligence could cripple your brand before you've even had a chance to generate it.

The question is, how much of your role plays to your strengths and personal brand, and how much are just chores? If the thing you're best at only represents 5% of your day, then you need a better system to allow you to play to your strengths.

Can you hire a part-time assistant? Can you make your business more efficient? City of Hope Hospitals designed a system where all their surgeons get to perform surgery as much as possible. This means they're not bogged down with admin or paperwork.

I've seen top professionals who excel in their roles hire assistants or junior partners who complement their skill sets — indeed, they relish the parts of the job that the top professional hates. This shedding of duties is only possible when you're clear on where you do your best work.

> ### CASE STUDY: Owning your approach
>
> When I started an internet company, one of the lead venture capitalists told me he did not write or read his emails. He had an assistant do it.
>
> He said, "I get paid tens of thousands of dollars an hour to do one thing better than anybody else, and that's to ask questions. I am a professional question-asker."
>
> And he was. He was also able to hire an assistant to do the small things he didn't like doing, so he could spend more time and energy on his best talents. He made a career out of being a question-asker.
>
> Notice you didn't hear him describe himself as a venture capitalist, lawyer or investor? He described himself by his approach. He knew — and owned — his Atomic Brand.

Still skeptical? If you're still saying to yourself, "This brand thing doesn't matter because no one cares about my approach, they just care about the results," then you've turned yourself into a function. You're simply a generic commodity — like the milk from Chapter 1. It's fine if people are familiar with your work and happy with the way you operate, but you're in danger of another brand coming along that your clients might try and like.

Think of your services like a car. Some people won't care about the make or model, as long as it goes. But then one day, they discover another car that gets really good mileage, it's cheaper to run and has a better warranty. This other car has differentiated itself from yours. Now, your functions are no longer special, and you're in danger of losing that customer forever.

You might also be saying to yourself, "I've been doing business for 15 or 20 years. It's working. Why do I need a brand?" If you're in the top of your field and you're happy with your results, then this system may not be for you.

You just need to hope a competitor doesn't get clear on their brand differentiation and take your business away. Microsoft did it to IBM. Senior successful people get replaced all the time by changes in management or business strategy. Technology can upend markets, such as travel and real estate and transportation. The world can be hit with an unprecedented financial crisis, pandemic or other paradigm shift.

Even if you are at the top and have been for years, it's helpful to know your brand. Being able to differentiate yourself from your competitors (and even your colleagues) gives you an edge. It also helps you stay relevant and current to your target audience.

Why describing your approach is not enough

At this point, you might be thinking, "Hey! I've got my personal brand now. I've got a commercial approach. Why do I need to keep reading? Why do I need to know what my inventory is?"

Your commercial approach describes how you will benefit your audience through your unique approach, ignoring any technical skills. But it's not enough — now you have to establish proof points to show you have the skills and attributes to back it up.

Your technical skill is something you pursue or do — and hopefully it's self-generated as a result of your natural, authentic brand and your personality or interests. By uniting your unique approach with your technical capabilities, we're blending your unconscious way of being with your conscious way of being. This makes your personal brand more deliberate and vastly more powerful, so you can own your brand rather than it owning you.

Your brand will help you get you an interview, the phone to ring, or someone to remember you. Put another way: it gets you in the door, but if you want to close the deal, you need to have an inventory.

An inventory is a unique set of skills and experiences that reinforce your unique approach and enhance your brand. You don't buy an Apple for its brand — you buy an Apple MacBook because you need a computer.

Conclusion

Now you've discovered more about your authentic self, including the habits and approaches that can make you a true asset to any company or client. Take a moment to look back at your exercise answers and continue to refine them.

Really. This pause is essential to help you test whether your first answers are a good fit. Think about it. Sleep on it. Walk on it. You'll be amazed where inspiration can strike.

Then, when you're ready, let's dive into the next chapter, which is all about discovering your passions that drive you further.

CHAPTER 5
Your approach is not enough without passion

Objectives

Yes, I know this part sounds a bit "soft-skills," "right-brained," or "emotional." But imagine how much easier — and more enjoyable — your life would be if your work aligned with your passions? It would feel so much less like work!

That's the goal. By the end of this chapter you will:

- Discover what you're passionate about.
- Understand how your passions can drive and motivate you.
- Use your passions to enhance your approach.
- Understand how to incorporate them into your brand.
- See how important your passions are to your journey of self-discovery.

My goal for you is to be as passionate about your brand as I am about helping you discover it. Let's continue moving to your next level.

Passion gives you life, and life gives you passion

The word *passion* means "a strong and barely containable emotion." Its origins go back to 1175, when it was first used in Old English to describe, "the passion of the Christ." In other words, Jesus's suffering. Since then, the meaning has expanded and morphed over time. But the crux of it is this: *passion is a thing you are willing to suffer for.* It's something you're willing to put a lot of energy and effort into, because you love it.

Passion doesn't have to be work related (we'll get to this in a bit). It could be your hobby or interest. It could be sports, politics, learning, entertainment, food, wine, health, fitness, reading, art, charities, music, travel — the list is endless! The point is that it's something (anything) you are driven to spend time and energy on.

For some people, this is work. Most of the people I know that have built net worths in excess of $50 million just love what they do and almost never stop. Like Tom Brady having a tough time quitting football, or Steven Spielberg still making movies well past a typical retirement age, these people are so in their groove they feel alive while delivering their brand. The list of examples of people extending their career because their passion is endless. They have enough money to retire in style and still choose not to. Why? Because they feel alive delivering on their passion.

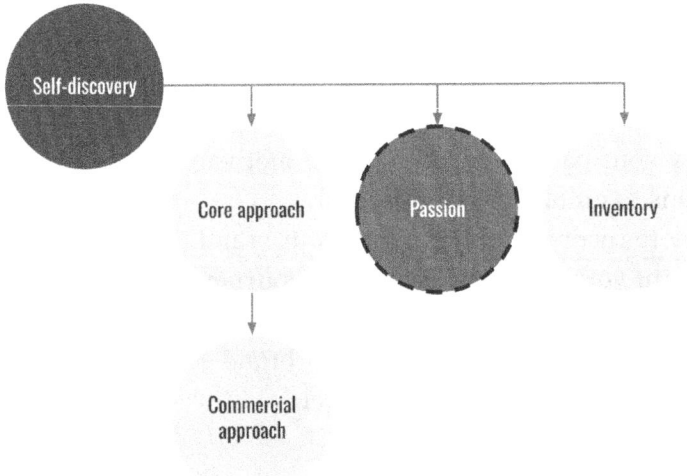

When a person can understand your context — your passions and what drives you — over your content — the work you do — it generates powerful trust. They believe you're willing to sacrifice for your mission and purpose. They understand what you have decided to be accountable to, and that is observed by a combination of looking at your passions, and the efforts and discipline you're willing to put into it.

Arnold Schwarzenegger was so passionate about body building he was willing to lift weights eight hours a day. For most people, spending that long in a gym is suffering. To him, that was his discipline in following his passion. By discipline, I mean a willingness to go deep to learn, study, practice and perfect a skill. A person in law school needs to be disciplined for law. The word "discipline" actually means to "be the disciple of." And discipline feels much less like work when it involves the things you're passionate about.

Share the love

If your passions are things that are not directly related to your work or job, that's okay. Sharing your passions with others can be a great way to connect and strengthen particular relationships, especially working relationships. A mutual passion for fishing, golf, art exhibitions, hiking, football, or charities can provide a great way to develop a more personal rapport with a client away from the office. The energy of a mutual passion can also generate energy within the relationship.

Yes, I'm talking about client and customer relationships, but the same applies to romantic or friendly relationships too.

> "There are 86,400 seconds in every day, how many of those seconds do you spend on your passion?"
> — Helen Robbins

What if you don't have a passion?

This world seems built for people who are driven. They have their unique approach, skills and career trajectory nailed. Ever since I was in kindergarten, I can remember being asked what I wanted to be when I grew up ... the assumption being that I knew. I didn't. It changed constantly. And it did for most of my adult life.

After making some big changes in my career between industries (from commercial real estate, to a tech startup, to a global company, to business performance coaching), plus deep soul-searching and self-discovery, I was able to develop my brand and find a career that aligned with my passions.

If you don't feel like you have any strong passions and you don't really know what you want to be when you grow up, that's okay. You can still escape pigeon-holed clock-watching purgatory. Ask yourself: What are you strongly interested in?

What things do you spend most of your time and energy on? How much do you enjoy it? What things have you thought about pursuing but keep pushing down the priority list? If you're spending a lot of time on social media, what about it interests you? Is it travel photography? Other people's stories? Playing online games? Dig a little deeper.

If you don't have a particular passion, is there something you do that you spend a lot of time on? Say, if you are putting together a slideshow at work, do you spend a lot of time putting in photos or creating animations? If you're doing expenses — do you spend a lot of time sourcing receipts or cross-checking bank statements? Or are you more interested in knowing how to allocate a budget properly, so expenses don't balloon unexpectedly?

Be careful you do not mix up your passions with your natural drives, like eating, sleeping or sex. These are nature-driven and nature-supported, just like breathing, but they are things you will do no matter what, and nature is pushing you on them.

For example, if you're passionate about food — is it presentation, preparation, flavors, cultures? If it's just eating, then, unless you like writing food reviews, it might be more nature-driven. Passion is something that will drive your approach. Let's dig into that now.

EXERCISE 5.1: Finding your passions

List 10 of your passions. Remember, it can be anything. If you're not sure what your passions are, ask yourself: What is it in your life that you have the most energy for? What makes you feel rejuvenated? What need do you think it's filling?

_____   _____

_____   _____

_____   _____

_____   _____

_____   _____

Take a moment to **review these passions.** Are they activity based? Are they social? Do you actively take time to pursue them? Are there any common threads here? If there are commonalities, make a note. We'll come back to this.

EXERCISE 5.2: Doing your passions

Looking at your list above, circle one or two that you haven't done for a while. Guess what? Now you're going to do it. Okay, so maybe you're passionate about scuba diving and it's not something you can do locally — or can afford to do right now. But could you go for a swim in the ocean? Visit a local aquarium? If you're passionate about travel, but haven't been anywhere lately, plan a day trip somewhere local. Or even an afternoon's drive. Just take some time to explore and indulge yourself.

Your passion and hobbies can also involve group activities such as sports, club meetings, or volunteer work. Sometimes helping and interacting with others can also generate a feeling of personal satisfaction, while helping you to foster rewarding relationships.

Following your passions is important. I don't mean blindly pursuing your passions endlessly, at the expense of all else. I mean taking some time to indulge in your passions on a regular basis.

Why? We live and breathe for our passions. Remember — these are the things we're willing to expend energy for, even at a significant personal cost. These are the things we want to make time for.

When we do them, we feel happier and more energized, and this flows into all other aspects of our life, whether we recognize it consciously or not. Our passions spark joy and may help us access greater creativity or more balanced mental health. It is also a key in our personal branding.

Be honest with yourself about whether your passion is truly healthy. Addictions are different from passions. Make it a priority this week to indulge in a long-ignored passion and spark some extra joy in your life.

Make a note about how you feel after indulging. Did you have more energy, or feel more creative? Did you notice any difference in your interactions with work colleagues, clients or friends? Was there anything about the approach you took in indulging your passion that you also do in your work? Answers to these questions could be useful in helping you further refine your personal brand.

> **CASE STUDY: Connecting your passion to your vocation**
>
> When I was a kid, I loved going to sporting goods stores with my best friend, Todd. It started when we looked for skateboards and grew into all things sports related, like skiing, camping, and hiking.
>
> One day, I walked into a sporting goods store and asked the manager for a seasonal job during the busy Christmas shopping season. He asked me why he should hire me. I told him I'd been going to all the sporting stores in the area for years — and this one was by far the best. I told him why I thought so, based on my extensive personal research and natural curiosity. I told him I knew what people were looking for at other stores and that I knew how to show them our stock was better.
>
> He gave me the job. That season I was the number one salesperson by far — even though I also frequently referred customers to the other stores, as I knew what they carried.
>
> Customers kept telling my manager how good I was and why they would keep coming back to our store. Over the years I worked at the store, I became an expert on sports gear — and I kept learning so I could stay on top of the next-level gear.

The bottom line: What you're interested in can be leveraged. You just need to find the right places to do that.

You might notice when you reflect on your hobbies or passions that there are opportunities to use them more often in your work.

For example, my son was very passionate about video games. When I watched him play, I realized he put a lot of effort into coordinating everyone to get together and do a mission online. It dawned on me that these skills would really help him in other aspects of his life.

And it did. First, he became an Eagle Scout, then the event director for his fraternity, then he helped people advance into exclusive clubs. In the commercial world, he connected companies to help them build value together.

My son's brand is now "connecting growing companies with great real estate decisions for their business needs." Can you see his early passion brought to his present-day work? His coordinating skills came naturally from his passion for online gaming.

If you love football and know clients who love football games, you could invite them to the next game with you. Or if you're a passionate hiker, joining a hiking group might help you to expand your circle and find new potential clients.

Exploring your passions not only refuels your soul, but might also open up new unexpected opportunities for you too.

Be a willing learner

The things you are passionate about are the things you're willing to put more effort and energy into. They give you the motivation and drive to learn and advance your skills. On the emotional side, learning or studying more about what you're passionate about can generate intellectual drive and take you in new directions of discovery.

People are very attracted to enthusiasm and passion, so if they see you applying your intellect and passion to enrich your learning, it will enhance their experiences in dealing with you. It makes them want to hire you or use your products or services even more.

The bottom line is: Discover and explore your passions.

The most important concept here is to understand the driver underlying your favorite activities and passions. Once you've figured that out, you can apply it to other areas of your life. Look at the intention underlying the action — you might like gardening, but what you really like about it is making things orderly and pretty. You might enjoy chess, but digging deeper, it's really about strategy. For me, it started with sporting goods, which was fueled by my natural curiosity.

To be 95 percent more knowledgeable than 95 percent of the population on most subjects, all you have to do is read five books on it. That's a pretty small investment to "own" an expert position in a subject you're passionate about.

The difference between approach and intention

Approach is your baseline perspective or point of view.
It's the way you bring yourself to a situation, task, interaction or role.

Intention is the purpose of an action, decision or plan.
It is the trigger or motivation behind an action,
and produces goals, action or thinking.

Our approach is often so deeply embedded in our minds that it sits in our subconscious. You'll see this when you observe multiple people doing essentially the same job with the same intended goals — each individual will put their own personal touch on how they perform the task. That's their unconscious approach in action.

I discovered this phenomenon when I was working with 11 different managers in a region, all of whom held the same title and role in their respective offices. As I mentioned in a previous example, they all were charged with building the business in their regions as part of a global corporation. I found that each person tackled the job with a different set of methods, viewpoints, opinions, and values.

One of the managers operated strategically and was constantly trying to out-think the competition. Another was deeply connected to their community and sat on multiple boards, so leveraged those connections. Another manager was very good at amplifying their message to the market through earned media interviews. Another focused on building their team, working to improve skills and promote promising talent.

After working with these managers for years, it became clear that these habits governed how they approached all sorts of challenges. Even when they were trained and coached in another method, they couldn't produce results with as much success or enthusiasm as their natural approach. But for their natural approach, they each seemed to have an endless amount of energy.

As a regional leader, I would call the managers together for strategic planning, which required a ton of time and effort to outline a roadmap or implement a new system. We wanted the managers to align behind one way of doing things. And most of the projects we planned fell flat. There was initial enthusiasm, then disillusionment, then a search for the guilty, and finally praise for the non-participants. It was a frustrating time-suck that ultimately saw the managers go back to their old habits.

But then we tried a different approach. We declared a new future and waited to see who would show up, and what they would offer to contribute to get us there. In this experiment, no one was required to participate. No one was required to "align" and we weren't looking for "buy-in." It was a real choice.

I was astounded to see what happened. A few managers showed up and agreed with the intention — our declaration of a new future. Then more showed up, and they proposed ways to contribute that were consistent with their natural approaches. Despite the differences in individual approaches, they all had a common, shared intention. They saw momentum build and got excited about contributing to the project in their own way.

Our intention was a declaration of what we wanted the future to be, and the approach was an individual way of aligning with that intention.

Here's another example of the difference between intention and approach. I have an intention to go to Costco and get us stocked up at a good value. But my habit (my approach) is to be curious to find the next level in everything. So when I go to Costco I am always looking for next-level stuff. I can't help myself. This approach is just how I am.

When Candy Lightner started Mothers Against Drunk Driving (MADD), she had the intention to get drunk people off the road. Her approach was being a self-described "crusader with a purpose." She was a tireless and fearless consensus-builder, strategist and advocate. As her project expanded, she was named one of the most influential people in the twentieth century.

Unaware or aware, our approach will always show up. But when we are aware of our approach, it becomes much more powerful for our community. Why? Because other people we are working with will realize what's driving us.

EXERCISE 5.3: Where do you spend your time?

Draw a graph or make a note of where you spend most of your time. Can you carve out more time for your passions? Do you need to make more time for rewarding social activities that help you connect with people?

_____

_____

_____

_____

_____

_____

_____

_____

Conclusion

Chapter 5 is short on length, but big on impact. Take a moment to reflect:

- What did you learn about your passions and interests?
- How can these fuel what you do and how you do it?
- Are there opportunities to bring your passions into the workplace more or vice versa?
- How do your passions feed into your personal brand?

Next, we'll work on translating your passions into your résumé, by taking your personal inventory.

Before you move on...

In some activities, you might say that you're "in flow" or "in the zone." Time passes and you hardly notice. It's almost something you'd do for free because you have so much energy for it. (Some might even say you geek out on it.) What activities do you do where you find yourself in flow? This is a great way to reveal your natural approach.

CHAPTER 6
To the résumé — and beyond!

Objectives

By the end of this chapter, you'll be able to:

- Identify qualifications relevant to your brand.
- Understand how this becomes your inventory.
- Know the difference between your capabilities and credibility.
- Understand how your qualifications can reinforce your brand.
- Know how to mix everything you've learned in the last three chapters and apply them to your brand.

Taking your inventory

"I'm not what happened to me. I'm what I chose to become."
— Carl Jung

This is part of your process of self-discovery. Now you'll learn how to take your experience, skills and qualifications, mix them with your approach and passions to generate your own unique Atomic Brand.

Inventory is a unique set of skills and experiences
that reinforce your unique approach and enhance your brand.

This is where you get to put it all together. It might take time and it might take some refining. But give yourself a chance to play and have fun with it, so that you're open to exploring all the possibilities. When you finally put it together and it clicks for you, you'll have something powerful and effective.

Also remember: None of this is set in stone. You can always come back and refine this as new thoughts or ideas occur to you.

Now, let's get started. In the graph below, we're on the final pivotal point of your self-discovery journey: your inventory.

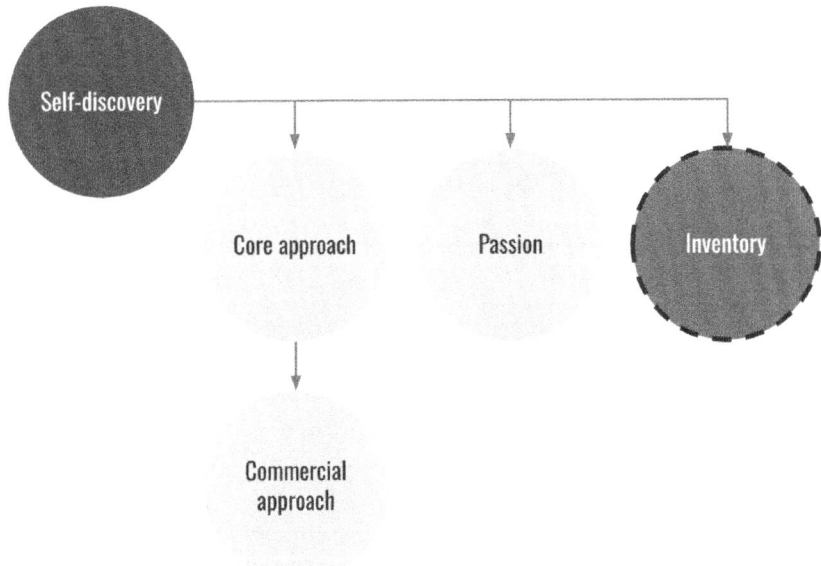

Your Qualifications

Your inventory is made up of your qualifications. These are things that you do, you know how to do, or you've done before. You probably naturally use your approach when you do these things.

We're not necessarily cataloging qualifications in the traditional sense. We want to unearth the unique skills and experiences you have that reinforce your personal brand.

Qualifications fall into two main categories:

- Capability
- Credibility

Capabilities

Capabilities are specific, demonstrable skills. Some are the kinds of things you would call out on a résumé. But if you can tell a story about how you've successfully applied it, it has potential for your personal brand.

For example, if you're extremely capable with Photoshop, how did you use this skill? What problem did you solve? Did you successfully use it to fix a printing error in time for publication and save your company money by avoiding reprinting or a re-shoot?

It's also important to think of your capabilities beyond the workplace. As an example, some of your capabilities might include:

- **Mental** — Are you able to concentrate for long periods of time? Function with little sleep? React calmly in a crisis?
- **Relational/social** — Are you a good icebreaker? Good at connecting like-minded people?
- **Physical** — Do you have a lot of energy? Uncommon stamina?
- **Managerial** — Are you good at making teams cohesive? Making sure everyone's on the same page? Good at organizing or assigning tasks?
- **Political** — Are you good at getting different groups of people together to make decisions? Are you diplomatic?
- **Linguistic** — Are you a good, clear communicator? Can you convey complex ideas in speech or writing?
- **Technical** — Can you adapt complicated language to common terms? Figure out complicated software quickly?
- **Health-related** — Do you understand good ergonomic practices? Know how to use proper breaks or daily schedules to maximize productivity?

Another way to think about capabilities is your expertise. Expertise is usually the result of a large amount of time devoted to study and practice. Like Tom Brady being a student of football, or Marie Curie, who won two Nobel prizes for her groundbreaking research on radioactivity. People who are passionate about what they do are usually the people willing to spend hours becoming an expert.

Some jobs lend themselves well to passion and expertise. It's easy to see why people devote their lives to carve out successful careers in sports, scientific research, journalism, or the arts. But what about other, less flashy jobs such as office management, HVAC installation, or working as a cashier or a receptionist? I've come across people passionate about all kinds of jobs — including these.

One time, a woman talked to me for 20 minutes about how some electrical subpanels were better than others. I once had a limo driver who prided himself on how smoothly he could drive in stop-and-go traffic. He was an expert driver, and his approach was being smooth. The funny thing was his whole life was like that: smooth and calm.

Sometimes we make excuses for our passions and the time we spend on them. But there is a competitive advantage to developing expertise in something you're passionate about. It can be a great way to differentiate yourself from others. There simply aren't as many people who operate at the expert level — and it's harder to achieve than people think.

Does building expertise require 10,000 hours, as some books claim? Will it take 10 years at school, or 10 years of apprenticeship under an amazing mentor? In a very small market, you might be able to build expertise that exceeds anyone else very quickly. In a large market, it depends on how many others are doing it and how well known you are. If this is the case, you will have to further differentiate your brand. The key here is to apply your capabilities and expertise to your personal brand.

CASE STUDY: Finding a unique selling point

Naomi was a Pilates instructor who recently moved to Los Angeles to establish her own business. However, Pilates instructors in LA were a dime a dozen. Naomi realized her qualifications were unique because she had actually studied and received qualifications from Pilate himself.

As a result, she was able to offer a level of teaching that few could — undiluted, pure Pilates as created and taught by the original founder. This not only gave her a unique selling point in a heavily competitive market, it reinforced her brand of "Pure Pilates."

Interestingly, Naomi's concept of pure applied to many other areas of her life, including eating, gardening and self-care. It's another example of how an approach reaches into all areas of life, sometimes without any conscious design.

EXERCISE 6.1: Discovering your capabilities

List your capabilities. Try to write down as many as you can. It's important to think outside the box. Beyond your immediate work experiences and education, consider capabilities that might show through your hobbies, social clubs, achievements, and way of living.

Dig out your résumé. Review your capabilities on it and compare it to the ones you've just written.

- What needs to be updated?
- How can you apply your unique approach to your qualifications?
- How can you frame them to immediately reflect your brand?

_____

_____

_____

_____

_____

_____

_____

_____

_____

_____

_____

_____

Credibility and credentials

Credibility is defined as the quality of being trusted and believed in. The Latin root is the same as credentials: *credibilis* literally means "worthy to be believed."

Credentials include your education, certifications, and significant experience. These are the concrete and measurable examples of your accomplishments — they define your credibility, or make your claim of expertise believable. For example, if you're a doctor, you'll need a medical degree to be credible. Many professionals need specific licenses or accreditations.

Consider some of the following:

- Country or region in which you studied
- University degree
- Relevant major(s) or emphasis
- Noted professors with whom you studied
- Religious training
- School ranking
- Ranking in your specific field
- School reputation (e.g. a small liberal arts college known for academic rigor, versus a big state school known for athletics)
- Sports you played and the level you achieved
- Fraternity/sorority or club affiliation
- Extracurricular activities
- Work experience during school (on campus)
- Awards, commendations, and major achievements
- Special designations
- Acknowledgments
- Competitions in which you participated
- Thesis or advanced degree research topics
- Continuing education

Now let's expand this concept. Outside of your traditional education, let's consider your credentials as any experience, training, or form of education you've had that helped you to develop your unique skill set. What concrete examples can you think of that would make you credible? These could also include:

- Industry certifications or licenses
- Technical certifications
- Memberships
- Governmental — military service, security clearance, office held
- Citizenship
- Volunteer work

These are just ideas to help you consider all of the facets of your experience.

EXERCISE 6.2: Discovering your credentials

List whatever credentials you have. List all of them, not just what's on your current résumé. Ask: What have you learned or done that got you to where you are today?

_____

_____

_____

_____

_____

_____

_____

_____

> **CASE STUDY: Lessons that weave through a career**
>
> I once worked with a CEO who considered his experience as working the night shift at Denny's for years to be the most valuable service training in his career. Why? He learned that he had great people skills and honed them by dealing with all kinds of customers.
>
> When a tough-looking motorcycle gang came in, no one wanted to approach them, so they sent in the new guy. He learned how to treat even the scariest-looking customers. He also learned how to keep staff motivated and how to handle tricky situations with minimal staff.
>
> These lessons on service and making friends stuck with him throughout his career. He applied these skills to his CEO tenure — making his focus "servant leadership." As a result, he was hugely popular with his employees.

When you really think hard about discovering your credentials, you should come to the conclusion that there is more to the picture of you than a plain old résumé.

A key element in uncovering your unique brand is thinking beyond what would be on a traditional résumé to consider all of the experiences that make you, you. These have helped you crystallize your approach and inspired you to follow your passions. They're also entirely unique to you.

They could include:

- Cultural or ethnic background
- Languages you speak
- Where you've lived
- Relevant travel
- Specific achievements outside of work (climbing a major mountain, winning a competition, or simply striving as a competitor)
- Companies worked for; positions held
- Major work projects, accomplishments and innovations (including patents or intellectual property)
- Volunteer experience
- Board member service

- Family
- Cultural milestones (e.g. "I was at Woodstock.")
- Hobbies & interests
- Publications and presentations
- Client list
- Unique claim to fame — struck by lightning, on a TV show, made a discovery
- Major challenges overcome
- Social media achievements and influence

Here are some useful examples of some people who've built a personal brand:

- **Jim Cramer**, who hosts the "Mad Money" podcasts and is part of CNBC's financial team, is an expert on the stock market. He differentiates himself by appealing to retail investors (average people without huge capital) — his brand is about helping everyday people make money through investing.

- **A shuttle bus driver** specialized in doing an informational presentation from a comedic angle while taking you from the airport to your rental car.

- Similarly, **an airport aide** who pushed passengers in wheelchairs around the terminal ended each ride with a short but incredibly beautiful serenade (passengers all around clapped).

- **A shoe-shine guy** at Seattle's SeaTac airport was known as a philosopher who'd have great inspirational conversations with his customers while polishing their shoes.

You're qualified. So what?

Now, you've got your big list of qualifications. Great. Now we need to whittle them down. Why? Three big reasons:

- **Relevance**: If your qualifications and skills aren't useful to your potential clients or customers, why should they care? Sure, you might have been a national spelling bee finalist five times, but unless part of your personal brand is being an excellent proofreader, nobody cares. (Okay, maybe your mom cares.)

- **Audience or situation**: You also need to know who you're targeting to ensure your unique qualifications are relevant to them. While this is about relevance, it's more specific. You want to be relevant to your specific target audience. The fact that I've been to San Diego Comic-Con every year since 1972 might not have a big payoff in my real estate organization. But it might be relevant if I was working for Max or Netflix, and it would absolutely be relevant if I worked for SYFY, the science fiction channel.

- **Domain**: Think of this as the industry or area of influence you're targeting. If your goal is to work within a particular industry, then some of your qualifications need to relate to it.

We'll discuss how to apply your unique qualifications to reel in your dream client or dream job in the next section.

EXERCISE 6.3: Your unique experiences

List 10 of your experiences outside of education and training. These might include places you travel, your cultural or ethnic background, your special achievements, and perhaps even your passions.

_____   _____

_____   _____

_____   _____

_____   _____

Did any of these help you form your unique approach? Conversely, how does your unique approach help you to achieve or access these experiences?

EXERCISE 6.4: Create your own commercial

Create your own promotional commercial. **Start by filling in each of the elements below.**

- Commercialized approach _____

- Domain or audience _____

- Ideal client situation _____

- Example result/achievement _____

- Action step _____

Now, you can mix them in any order. Make it as catchy and exciting as you can. This is your chance to tell them not only what you do, but also the way you approach it. You'll also tell them what you believe related to your approach, what kinds of clients you serve, and some of the results you've achieved. This shows why people should believe in and value your qualifications:

_____

_____

_____

_____

_____

_____

_____

Here's my 30-second example statement:

> Hi, I'm Craig Robbins and I'm a business performance coach. I help ambitious people take their business performance to the next level. I do this with a unique set of counterintuitive tools that accelerate your business with less stress, effort and wasted time. I do this for clients all over the world, large and small. My clients report gains of 40% to 400% within year of working with me.

Now it's time to apply your commercial in real life. Let's pretend you have just met someone and they want to hear about what you do.

Practice is everything to help you gain confidence, polish, and continuously refine your commercial. So take a moment to **write down five people** who are not family members, who **you could call up and practice** your 30-second commercial with. You'll ask them to listen to it and then provide honest feedback on anything that doesn't make sense or doesn't feel authentic to who you are.

_____

_____

_____

_____

_____

When they say, "Tell me more…"

The purpose of a commercial is not to answer all the questions a potential client might have. Instead, its purpose is to inspire questions. People who hear my 30-second commercial might then ask, "What does the next level mean?" "What kinds of counterintuitive tools do you use?" or "Have you worked with clients in my industry or with my specific problem?"

That's why you'll want to develop two versions of your commercial: a 30-second version that you just worked on in this exercise, and an extended version — typically prompted when they say "tell me more" — that takes about two to three minutes to share.

Here is an example of my longer version:

My name and what I do: Hi, I'm Craig Robbins and I'm a business performance coach. I specialize in making space for people to go to their next level.

My commercial approach: I do this with a set of tools I've gathered and developed from some of the best businesses, professionals, professors, leaders and consultants from around the world. These tools help you accelerate your success with less stress, effort and wasted time.

Domain: I do this for ambitious business people who want to get to their next level faster, with less stress. This includes CEOs, executives, professionals, managers and even people in the beginning of their careers. They represent virtually every industry, including law, finance, insurance, real estate, doctors, charities and even politicians. Some of my well-known clients include Coca-Cola, GE, CBRE, Colliers International, City of Hope and many smaller ambitious companies and practices.

Ideal client situation: My ideal client is someone who is looking for their next level and can't seem to find the path to it. They want to go faster or want to learn new ideas to see if there is a next level for them. They need to be ambitious, coachable and able to manage themselves to use these tools.

Example results/achievement: I used these tools at Colliers International to start a corporate university. The participants achieved an average 67% increase in their individual revenue within one year.

After you've developed a longer version of your commercial, you'll ask for an action step. What do you want to happen next as a result of this person hearing about what you offer? Here are some examples...

1. If you know anybody who might be able to use me...
2. If you would like to sit down and find out more...
3. If you have an issue, let's see if I have something to help...
4. I am happy to be here and looking forward to meeting you...

Now combine the action step with your long-form commercial. Practice in the mirror, then with a trusted friend or colleague from your list above. Listen carefully to your friend's feedback and consider revising your commercial if anything feels awkward or out of place. You should be able to get to a point where this feels easy, authentic, and true to you.

EXERCISE 6.5: Fill in the blanks

If creating a short commercial feels too hard, **try filling in the blanks on the simpler version below.**

You know how … _____ ?
(State a problem experienced by the kind of people you help.)

My solution to that is _____

And an example is _____

Here's my example:

You know how people feel like they are stuck in their jobs and not doing what they're passionate about?

My solution to that is to help them identify who they naturally are, and then develop that into a personal brand that helps them stand out.

For example, I coached a magazine publisher who is a competitive runner. He learned that he could "get more out of himself running," by helping companies who advertise in his magazines to get more from their advertising dollars.

> ### CASE STUDY: Reframing your value to pique interest
>
> A friend is a cold-call coach. He trains people on how to make cold calls, but he found it difficult to engage people's interest when he told them about his practice. That's because most people have an aversion to telemarketing and cold calls.
>
> At a party one night, in a burst of frustration, he blurted out, "I basically help people get to decision-makers." Instantly, the party-goer handed him a business card and told him to call them the next day. This connection led to thousands of dollars of repeat business.
>
> By reframing his value in a catchy way that clearly and directly benefited the client, he made his skills more desirable. That was how he built his brand.

Applying Atomic Brand rules

Now that you understand what your Atomic Brand is, here's a more concise summary of some of the main points we've discussed. It might be helpful to copy this and stick it on a wall somewhere, so you can refer to it. Ask yourself whether your brand fulfills all of the criteria below.

What is your Atomic Brand?
(Defining it)

It must be **authentic** to who you are, your authentic passions and expertise, and how you naturally operate (your approach).

It is based on your **unique approach** combined with a skill. Your approach will affect your use and delivery of that skill, and that will deliver your results. This is the recipe for a defining career.

> The approach component of the Atomic Brand will likely be **consistent** across home, work, social groups, and all other aspects of your life.

It should take a **unique position** in the market compared to others. Positive or negative, it doesn't matter — as long as you deliver on a promise that your market wants.

It should offer an obvious **commercial benefit** to your target market.

It is **not a slogan** or symbol, or just your name, unless you can make your name or symbol synonymous with what you deliver.

It is what **other people think** it is. For now. (That's the bad news. The good news is that you can influence your Atomic Brand to grow from here forward.)

How does your Atomic Brand grow?
(Managing it)

If you don't **manage** your brand, someone else will — unless they don't think about you at all.

Your brand **grows** when you help people get what they want, or get it faster.

Your brand **grows** when you keep your brand promise, which is the offer you make to your market.

> Your brand **erodes** when you fail to deliver on your brand promise or you do something inconsistent with your brand.

Your brand **grows** when you help others grow their personal brands.

To succeed, **others** must want your Atomic Brand to succeed.

Your target **market will decide** if your brand message is working.

Measuring your results will show whether your brand is working. Be willing to tailor your message to get the desired results — but keep your approach consistent.

Conclusion

By now, you have a thorough understanding of your Atomic Brand. More specifically, you've learned how your unique approach, passions, qualifications, and experiences all fit together to form this unique and authentic brand that is 100 percent you.

But you're not done yet. Identifying your unique brand is only part of the story. To be effective, a strong brand must be received and recognized by an audience.

In the next phase of this book, we'll identify your audience. This helps your brand be appropriate to the situation at hand. If your brand doesn't solve an immediate problem for your target audience, then they're not going to pay for what you're offering.

The trick with branding is to frame your offer in a way that makes your brand seem essential to a specific set of people. Disney would not exist without families wanting wholesome entertainment they can all enjoy. Gucci wouldn't exist without people willing to spend big bucks on designer products to achieve "status." And that's where the following chapters come in.

You might find as you continue on this Atomic Branding journey that your personal brand becomes more and more niche as time progresses. That's OK, and your finely tuned brand might turn out to be even more effective. You can always revisit chapters or rework the exercises from the beginning to fine tune your message. In fact, I hope you do.

Now let's review what you've learned in this section.

- Do you have a clear understanding of what your personal brand is now?
- Do you understand how to apply your capabilities and credentials to it, to make you seem essential to your target audience?

Remember — it doesn't have to be perfect. It's a work in progress. Take all the time you need.

CHAPTER 7
Connecting with your audience

Objectives

By the end of this chapter, you'll understand:

- Who your current clients are.
- Who your ideal clients are, and therefore, your target audience.
- How people who know you well can help you reach your target audience.
- The main industry or domain of your ideal clients.
- Who to approach and target within your domain.

Your target audience is the people who will ideally use your services or product. The key here is to get as specific as possible. The more a target audience member feels like you are talking to and connecting directly with them, and the more you can specifically show how you'll help get them what they want, the stronger your brand equity will be. Hopefully, you'll be excited as you form a list of priority contacts!

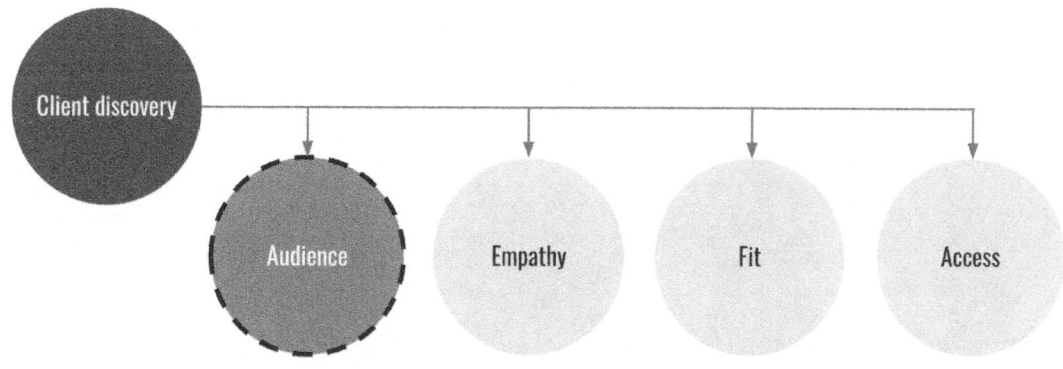

Client discovery

For your brand to be effective, you have to understand that you're targeting a specific group of people. Your brand only works if you evoke a response from your specific target group. If that group is too small, your client base won't be large enough to feed you. Too big, and you'll end up spending a fortune trying to advertise to a huge market, many of whom aren't your ideal customer.

As we move through this chapter, your approach will help you better align with and attract your target audience. But first, we need to figure out who your target client is, and how you'll engage with them. As you acquire your early customers, you'll learn more about what matters to them, and that might suggest that you modify your offer. For example, you might find out that your target customers aren't interested in your original pitch.

I saw this in action when I was targeting large insurance companies that were institutional owners of commercial real estate. Up to that point, I'd been targeting local owners and developers, whose main focus was to build wealth and make money. But when I took that offer to the institutional investors, it fell flat. Why? They didn't care so much about "building wealth" as they cared about avoiding risk. After all, they were insurance companies.

So at that point, I had to make an adjustment to my offer to deliver what the target market really valued. My approach stayed the same: I wanted to take my clients to the next level. For institutional investors, they wanted next-level safety, security and structure. That's how I adapted my offer.

For people who aren't targeting business clients — maybe your target market is your boss, coworkers or church group — this is relevant too. Adapting your offer is necessary for any group with whom you want to build your Atomic Brand.

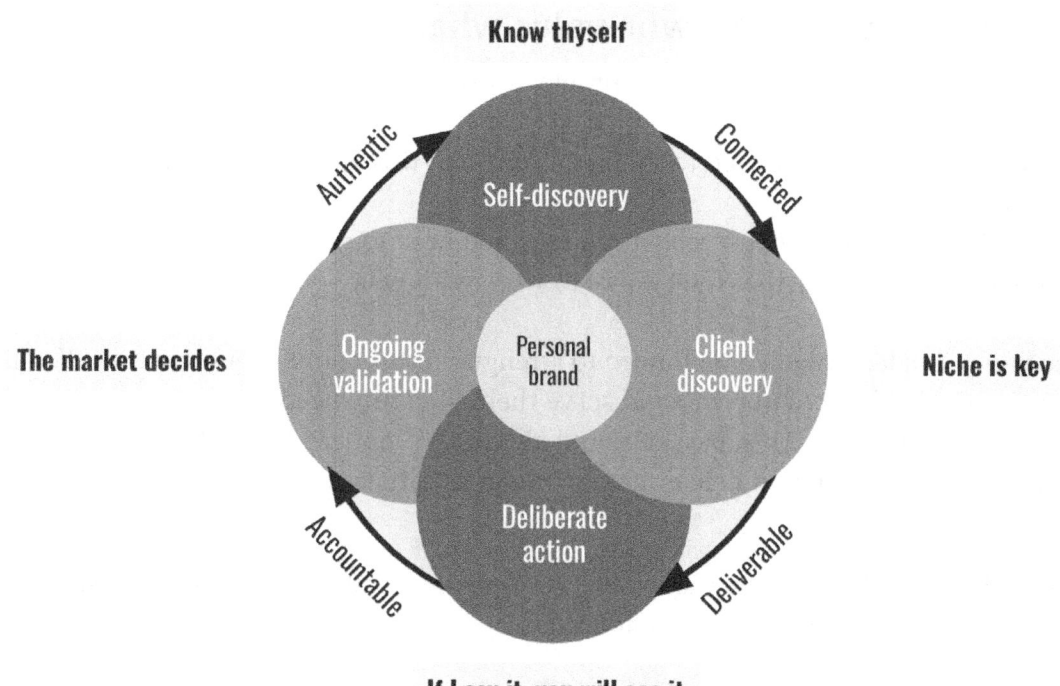

Client discovery is a key element in completing your Atomic Brand. It helps you understand:

- Who is already listening?
- Who do you want to listen?
- Why would they care?
- Would you be happy working with them, and they with you?
- Do you have access to them?
- How will they benefit from you?

Once you understand these fundamentals, it will become easier to use your brand to engage with them. I want you to pick clients who value what you have to offer. If you do that, you'll find prospecting effortless, because you're being the best you. You're a natural.

How do you pick clients who value what you offer?

- They are not merely people with a problem — they are people with the problem that you want to solve.
- You have a unique approach to their problem, and this approach will add value to your solution.
- They have identified their problem, so now you need to get their attention long enough to decide whether they'd like to work with you.

Once you've landed a client, you'll need to strengthen this connection over time. You'll be on an ongoing hunt to uncover and serve their changing needs. To achieve this, you'll use your natural skills, passions, and abilities to connect. This attention, which is true client engagement, will deliver greater client loyalty and ultimately, greater revenue.

Look at the image below. Client discovery involves the combining of several elements. We're going to focus on one element at a time.

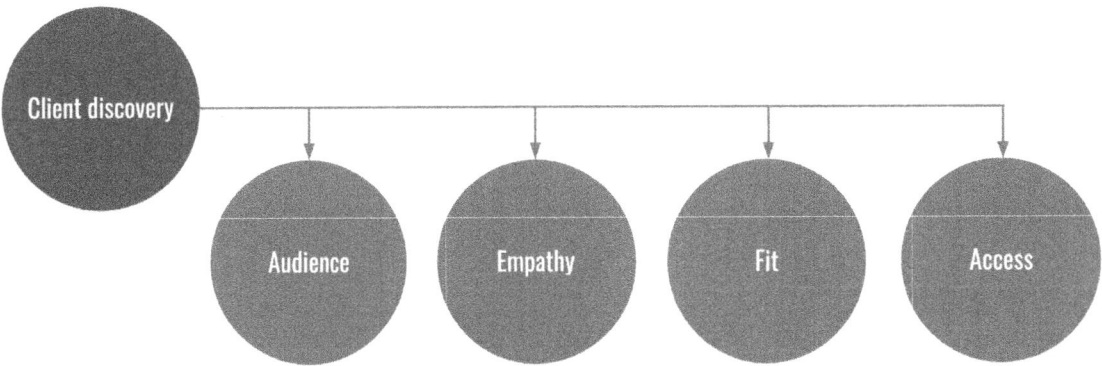

Now an important note here, when I'm talking about engaging a client, I'm not talking about referrals — simply passing on a name and phone number and then moving on. My goal for you is long-lasting connections that generate repeat business. To achieve this, you need to understand how to use your natural skills, passions, and abilities to connect with the right clients for you.

Working with the right clients makes a big difference.

EXERCISE 7.1: Who knows your approach?

From the exercises you completed in Chapter 4 (see: "Finding your approach" and "Action phrases"), **list who you usually share your approach with.**

Don't just say, "I do this for everybody" — that list is too large. Break down the big list of people into more specific groups.

For example, if you consider yourself analytical, do you help your friends analyze decisions they have to make? Do they feel better with your help? What specifically do they get from your interaction? Which friends do you help with your analysis? Who else benefits from your analytical approach?

_____

_____

_____

_____

_____

_____

_____

_____

EXERCISE 7.2: Discovering your target audience

Now let's narrow your target audience even further. Who are your dream clients, bosses, or customers? Notice I am not saying companies. Companies are just people working together with common goals. Who should know about your brand? Who are you trying to work with?

Consider the following:

- Customers
- Clients
- Partners
- Bosses
- Coworkers
- CEOs, HR managers, department managers, etc.
- Connectors: people who might refer or recommend you

Do any of these apply? **List them too. Group them together where appropriate.**

Now, order and group the above by the most important and desirable targets first.

GROUP A: _____
_____
_____
_____

GROUP B: _____
_____
_____
_____

GROUP C: _____
_____
_____
_____

GROUP D: _____
_____
_____
_____

EXERCISE 7.3: Narrowing your target audience

Now, let's narrow down your target audience even further. **Ask yourself the following questions and write down your answers.** Refer to your answers from the previous exercise and see if you can get more specific. As before, group them where appropriate.

- What need would the person you're working with have that relates to what you provide? This could be a coworker, client, boss — anyone you think would be involved in the area where you want to build your personal brand.

- Where are they now in their quest, and where do they want to be in the future? Do you have the tools to get them there?

- Where is your target audience on the way to solving their problem? Are they unaware of the problem; aware of the problem but unaware of potential solutions; or aware of solutions but unsure which option to pursue? Who are the decision-makers, influencers and advisors to these people?

- Do you like these people enough to spend a career working with them?

- Do you have the skills, finesse and social capital to spend considerable time with them?

- Do you have access to them? Or, do you know someone who has access or influence over them?

- Are there a lot of them or few?

- Do you know how and where to source a contact list of these people?

- Are their issues recurring or are they a one-time event? If their problem generally occurs just once, you might need a broader list. If the problem is recurring, you will need to maintain your list through continued contact.

The key here is to narrow, narrow, narrow down your list. **Make it shorter if you can.** Ask yourself if you fully understand their situation and the issues they currently face.

Features and benefits

Features describe the attributes, skills, and functions of your product or service.

Features might describe the physical product, or the approach to creating or delivering the product or service.

Benefits are the tangible, valuable outcomes the target audience receives as a result of buying, using or experiencing the product or service.

Benefits might also include how you'll be satisfied, entertained or more comfortable as a result of the product.

So, while a feature describes an aspect of the product, a benefit describes how it delivers satisfaction. Put another way, if I don't get anything out of it, it's a feature; if I get something, it becomes a benefit.

Many people think they can just bring up a feature and the listener will intuit the benefit. But that doesn't always happen. That's why you need to be sure your message includes not only the features of your product or service, but the tangible benefits as well.

Let's look at some examples of feature/ benefit pairings.

- Feature: A car radio includes Sirius XM.
- Benefit: Sirius XM entertains the driver and helps them pass the time.
- Feature: Your doctor has a diploma on the wall that shows she went to a great school and has advanced training in solving your medical problem.
- Benefit: You have greater confidence that your doctor's qualifications and experience will create better outcomes in your health care.
- Feature: I'm going to cook your steak in a super-hot oven on cast iron.
- Benefit: Your steak will be incredibly tender and tasty.

But not all benefits are created equal. They require the context of the receiver — that person gets to decide whether it is a benefit to them.

- What is the benefit of Sirius XM to a deaf person?
- What is the benefit of your doctor's training to a person who doesn't have your medical problem?
- What is the benefit of the steak's preparation to a vegetarian?

> ### CASE STUDY: Is handmade a feature, benefit or neither?
>
> I went to the Porsche factory in 1980 for a tour. During the tour, Porsche representatives went on and on about how most of their cars were handmade — and they juxtaposed this quality against mass production, which they implied was sloppy and cheap.
>
> From Porsche's perspective, the emphasis on "handmade" showed exclusivity, craftsmanship and quality. But that didn't appeal to me. Handmade, to me, suggested there were variations in the manufacturing, that maintenance could be a problem, and that parts might be difficult to find.

To many people, handmade is considered the pinnacle of luxury, whether it's watches or handbags. But no one considers their technology "handmade" and in fact would probably avoid buying tech with human variances. All of this reveals that the feature of handmade will translate into a benefit for some people, and a liability for others. That's why it's so important to understand your audience's context with linking features with benefits.

The key takeaway is that you need to make sure the features and benefits are clearly linked. And since you need to understand the context of the audience to ensure a benefit applies to them, our next exercise is all about that. It will help you better understand your audience's issues, wants and desires, so that you can better offer a solution.

EXERCISE 7.4: Identifying the benefits to your target audience

Select the most important group first and determine if they would benefit directly from your list of five approaches (from Chapter 4). Don't focus on what you do, but on the benefit they get from you. My answer looks like this:

Group __CEOs__

APPROACH: I BRING...	BENEFIT: THEY GET...
Curiosity	New ideas to use for the next level
Need to win	A winning strategy

Now work through your list of groups:

Group 1 ___

APPROACH	BENEFIT

Group 2 ___

APPROACH	BENEFIT

Group 3 _____

APPROACH	BENEFIT
_____	_____
_____	_____
_____	_____
_____	_____
_____	_____

Group 4 _____

APPROACH	BENEFIT
_____	_____
_____	_____
_____	_____
_____	_____
_____	_____

Group 5 _____

APPROACH	BENEFIT
_____	_____
_____	_____
_____	_____
_____	_____
_____	_____

EXERCISE 7.5: Telling your target audience

Take some time to write out how you would describe what you offer to one of your selected groups. Does it sound commercially viable? In this exercise, we're going to build the framework of a "commercial" for your services.

Here's my example: My target client is a businessperson looking for new ideas and perspective to help them achieve what they want more easily and efficiently. So, I might say my career has always been about applying my curiosity to the business problems my clients are having. This has led me to new perspectives, new answers, and new approaches. My clients regularly say this is next-level thinking, and that it achieves next-level results.

Let's break down the components of my description:

- Target client type: a businessperson
- Target client's needs: new ideas
- Target client's goal: achieve their business goals, more easily and efficiently
- My approach: curiosity
- Benefits of my approach: new perspectives, new answers, new approaches
- What my clients say about me: next-level thinking that achieves next-level results

Now, write yours below:

Target client type: _____

Target client's needs: _____

Target client's goal: _____

Your approach: _____

Benefits of your approach: _____

What clients say about you: _____

Expanding on that, you can do the same for the all of your target audience groups:

Group 1:

Target client type: _____

Target client's needs: _____

Target client's goal: _____

Your approach: _____

Benefits of your approach: _____

What clients say about you: _____

Group 2:

Target client type: _____

Target client's needs: _____

Target client's goal: _____

Your approach: _____

Benefits of your approach: _____

What clients say about you: _____

Group 3:

Target client type: _____

Target client's needs: _____

Target client's goal: _____

Your approach: _____

Benefits of your approach: _____

What clients say about you: _____

Group 4:

Target client type: _____

Target client's needs: _____

Target client's goal: _____

Your approach: _____

Benefits of your approach: _____

What clients say about you: _____

Group 5:

Target client type: _____

Target client's needs: _____

Target client's goal: _____

Your approach: _____

Benefits of your approach: _____

What clients say about you: _____

> **CASE STUDY: When clients have different needs**
>
> I had a client who sold insurance to companies. He told me, "I don't do anything special because all of my clients have different needs." He then went on to tell me he only worked within the medical community and focused on hospitals. When a hospital administrator moved to a new facility, they would often bring his services with them. That is how he expanded his business.
>
> What my client was really saying was that he had an excellent baseline understanding for his customers' specific needs. He could deliver solutions that made his clients look good, benefited the hospital, and built loyalty.

This is an example of a man with a brand who didn't know it. Many top people aren't good at explaining why they're successful, so they fall back on "I work hard, and my clients trust me."

In reality, this guy was a great listener, with a deep subject matter expertise in the field of medical facility insurance, so he was uniquely able to deliver customized insurance products for hospitals.

Imagine how much more powerful this man's brand could be if he could articulate it and put it in commercial terms — meaning, position what he offers in a way that focuses on the benefit to the client. You just completed an exercise to help you be able to articulate your brand offer when you next have an opportunity.

> **"When given the chance to speak, speak your offer."**
> **— John Cundiff**

And when you get an opportunity, don't waste that chance! Writing out and practicing your personal brand will help you be ready. Then it will take some personal courage to start sharing what you've come up with. But don't worry … even if it doesn't feel natural immediately, with practice you'll find the words that fit, and you'll be encouraged by the response your brand generates.

EXERCISE 7.6: Adapting your commercial to your target audience

Look at your commercial from the last exercise. Did you notice how you had to modify the benefits for each group? Even if you describe the same feature to multiple audiences, you might describe different benefits from group to group, depending on your target audience's needs.

Write down the key benefits that you offer.

_____

_____

_____

_____

_____

_____

_____

_____

_____

Benefits come in many shapes and sizes. For example, objective, measurable benefits:

- Solve a defined problem
- Lower costs, less waste
- Increase sales
- Increase employee participation
- Reduce time to market
- Increase impressions, clicks, or a specific action
- Fewer errors
- Increase customer loyalty or repurchase
- The "proven" solution, backed by data, so I don't get in trouble if it goes wrong

Intangible or subjective benefits look more like these:

- Make a process easier
- Make me or my department look good
- Help my boss understand
- Change minds
- Help me feel better
- Reduce worry or risk
- Protect me or my team
- The "obvious" or "safe" choice, so I don't get in trouble if it goes wrong

I have found that intangible benefits are often more powerful than tangible benefits, but it takes time and trust to see it.

> ### CASE STUDY: Don't just ask for any job, focus on the benefit to them
>
> When I was at UCLA studying economics, a professor told me that a lot of people got jobs during the Great Depression. At the time, I thought a huge number lost their jobs and almost no one got hired unless it was for low pay, or government sponsored.
>
> My professor explained that the people who got jobs had one thing in common. They didn't ask potential employers, "Do you have any job openings? I will do anything." Instead, they said things like, "I see your business isn't established in Georgia yet. I'd be happy to open up that market for you. I am really good at starting things, building interest, and building a team."
>
> In other words, they showed how their unique approach and skills would directly and tangibly benefit their prospective employer.

Another way to identify your target audience

Thinking of a brand as a badge is another way to help you narrow down your target audience. This exercise might feel repetitive, but I find that sometimes doing the same thing a different way can unlock my brain and lead to unexpected results.

If you consider a brand to be a badge of trust, then your current audience — your current clients, coworkers, people you know well — are potential wearers of your badge. Your goal is for more of your ideal clients to buy and proudly wear your trust badge.

Trust is built on both having high influence and high familiarity. Your spouse, partner, best friend and best clients trust you because they know you. Hopefully, they listen to you.

That's what your personal brand is: a promise to your audience based on them trusting you. Except this time, your potential audience doesn't have to know you personally. They're familiar with you, they're influenced by you — without you even knowing them.

A high level of trust means you're pre-sold.

In other words, you don't need to convince them anymore. And when they tell a friend about you, you don't need to convince them as much to gain an opportunity with them.

People often call this a "referral-based roadmap" because your high influence and high familiarity enables people to pre-sell you to other people who know and trust them. They can say to their friends or clients, "You should use X for their X services because their approach has gotten me excellent results." This is a clear example of someone wearing your badge. This also links back to Chapters 1–3 where we talked about your brand promise.

The influence and familiarity grid

Let's put this level of "trust" on a grid so we can visualize it more clearly:

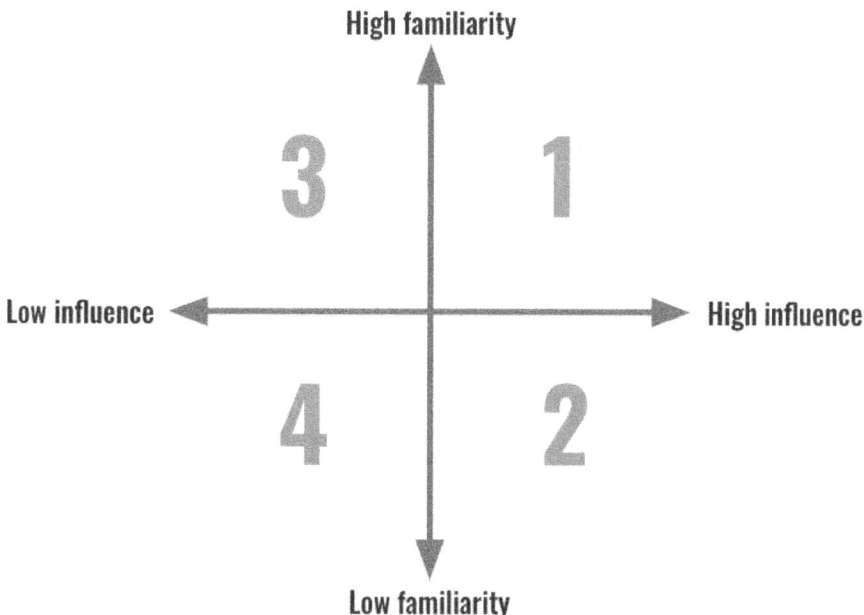

High familiarity means I know them, and they know you. Your mom has high familiarity with you, and so does your best client, boss (hopefully), and best friend. Low familiarity is someone who does not know you.

As for influence, this is the amount that a person holds power to sway attitudes and choices in a given situation, business, or industry. Jeff Bezos carries a high influence in the online retail world and at Amazon, but because you probably don't know him personally, he has low familiarity for you.

This makes Box 1 our sweet spot — high familiarity paired with high influence — whereas Box 4 is our lowest level target. Box 1 is where we want to move all of our people in our target market. These people are a valuable asset to you, just like your skills are an asset. So if you add in your personal brand, your credentials and your Box 1 people, you have the elements you need to get you where you want to go.

Think about people you know or interact with regularly. **What level of familiarity or influence do you have with them?**

Family members are obviously highly familiar. But many of these people don't have a lot of business influence. Your older sibling probably thinks of you as the annoying kid who just wants to play video games all day — not as an experienced business operator. They're unlikely to listen to your business smarts unless you've already got a substantial track record.

Also, they probably don't run in the business circles you want to be associated with. That said, just because they're highly familiar and have low influence, doesn't mean they can't contribute in some way. Don't discount them! You never know who they will come across, or what connections they could potentially make for you.

So back to the top right square. Who makes up your "Box 1"? Let's expand this and give it real values in the next exercise.

EXERCISE 7.7: Filling Box 1

Using the graph below, **write down your high influence and high-familiarity people**.

List them by their job position or relationship to you, not by their actual name. This isn't about a specific industry yet. It's simply a list of people who, in any organization, you would want to work with.

Who currently holds the key to using your brand or services? Think about:

- Your current clients
- Business partners and vendors
- Your boss or coworkers
- Industry group members
- Facebook groups.

Where do you have the most influence?

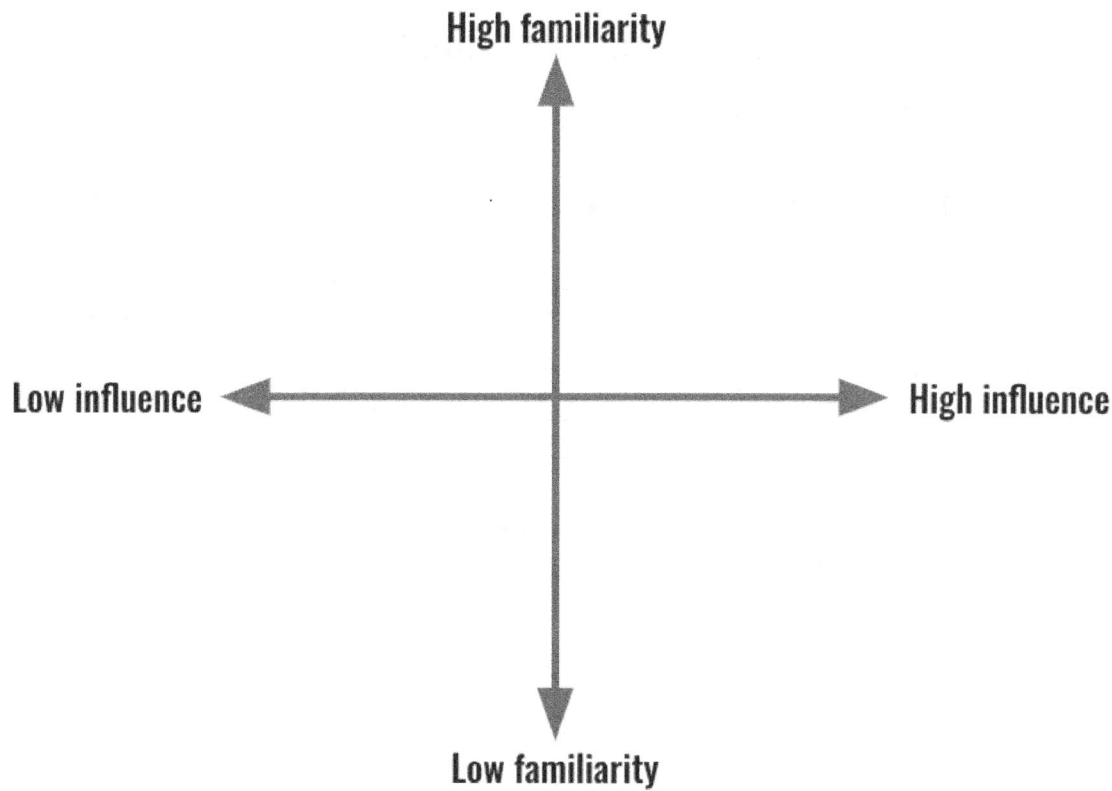

Your graph might look something like this:

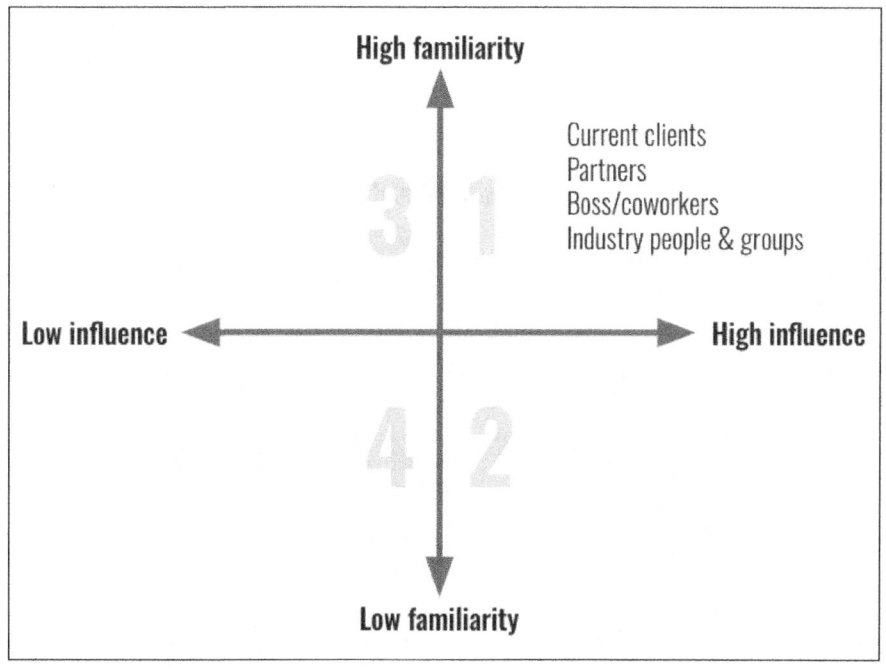

EXERCISE 7.8: Filling Box 2

Now let's work the bottom right corner — Box 2. Go back to the large grid from the previous exercise.

In Box 2, **add a list of potential contacts** that potentially have high influence but aren't familiar with you. These are potential clients, decision makers, key influencers, etc. They could be a human resource manager, a social influencer, the CEO or CFO. These are really your target audience. Specific names will help here, if you can.

Your mission is to get these people familiar with your brand. As they learn about you, you can move them into the top right square. As per below:

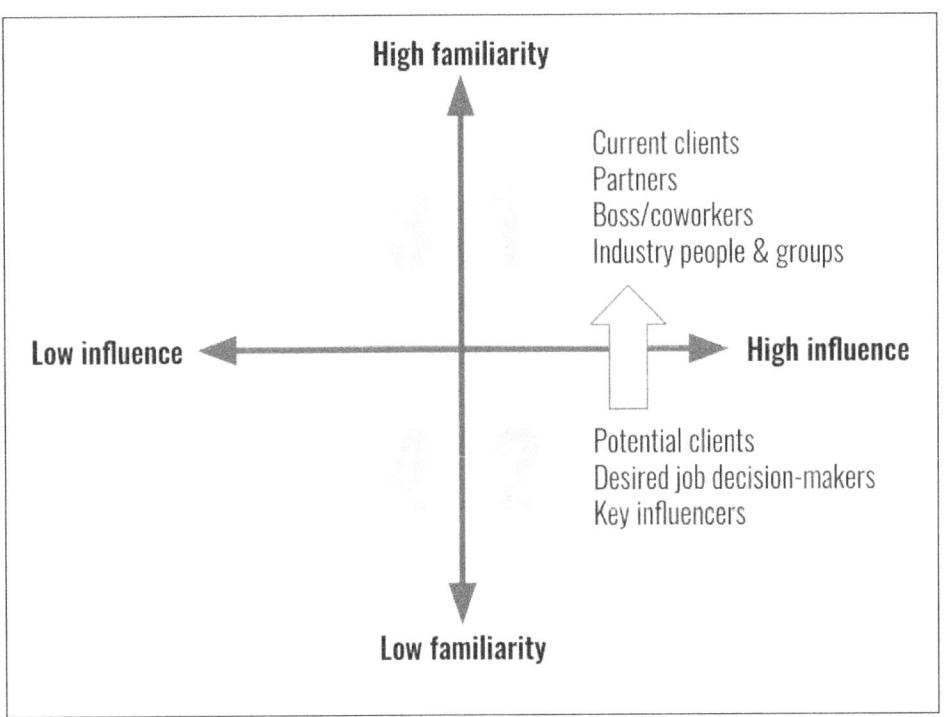

EXERCISE 7.9: Filling Box 3

Great! You've got two squares filled. Now let's go to Box 3 in the top left and complete that. Who are **people you're highly familiar with, but have low influence** with whom you want to build your identity? Is it family? Friends? People who follow you on Twitter (now called X)? A teacher at your kid's school?

I mentioned that these people might still be helpful if they know your brand. Take a moment to reflect on what you've filled in so far. The people in your top left square might be able to connect you with someone in your bottom right square.

Here's another example of that in action:

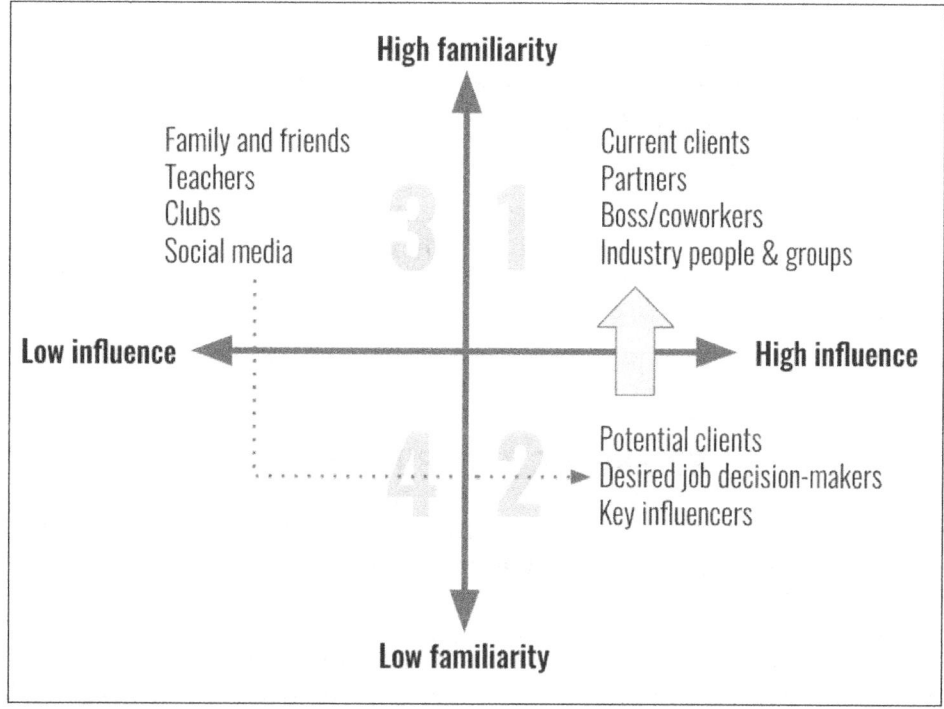

So many of my clients tell me their parents or kids have no idea about what they do. They tell their friends and acquaintances things like, "Our Kim is very busy at her job but she's very happy."

I teach my clients to make sure that the people who are most familiar with them know their brand so they can pass the message on. So the message becomes, "Our Kim has always been super creative, and she works at a print shop." When you get your personal brand and commercial approach figured out, the first people to test it on are your family members.

> ### CASE STUDY: Referral by accident
>
> My son accidentally referred a client to me when he was in fourth grade. He knew what I did (because, of course, I told him): "My dad sells big buildings." My son told his friend, who told his dad, who called me up to do some business.
>
> This is an example of low influence in my industry at the time, but high familiarity. And yes, I paid my son a referral fee at least 500 times over.

EXERCISE 7.10: Filling Box 4

Go back to your grid in exercise 7.7 and complete Box 4, the bottom-left square. These are **low influence and low familiarity people that you can really help**. You want them to know about your brand, but you don't have a direct connection to them.

Box 4 might seem like the hardest task but it's still worth doing. You might know someone in this area. Or, you might know someone who knows someone. You're probably not going to spend a lot of time filling in this box, but you never know. You might be at a house party one day and meet a friend of a friend who has a relationship with your Box 2 people.

EXERCISE 7.11: Linking them all together

Now you've completed the grid. This maps your target audience. When you look at this as a whole, ask yourself: Who can connect you with potential clients? Who do you know (or know of) who has the ability to make decisions and influence others?

If you can't link people directly from the top left grid to the bottom right, is there an intermediary person or job position that might be able to get you there? These are the people to add into the appropriate square.

Think of this exercise as a "Six Degrees of Separation" game for your career. **Who should I put on this grid, and who can help me reach them?** For example, if your best friend knows someone who works at Apple, can they find out the name of the person who runs the department you're trying to reach?

Be ready to call up the company directly to find out the information you need if they don't. You'll be amazed what you can discover once you overcome the initial fear of asking.

EXERCISE 7.12: Applying your domain

Now you have a list of job positions and relationships. Next, you'll narrow down your domain. If you imagine a target audience as an audience at a concert, your primary domain might be the front orchestra section, whereas the lesser targeted areas are on the balcony or sides.

Applying this to your personal brand, if you're a social media marketing whiz and you want to expand your client base, do you need to target more potential social media clients in the travel space? Are you looking for Instagram models? Are your qualifications more health-related?

Get really specific. The more specific you can get, the more you can appeal directly to your audience and the more engagement you will get. Write your specific domain here:

_____

_____

_____

_____

EXERCISE 7.13: Your priority contacts

Using your completed Familiarity/Influence grid, **fill in your list of priority contacts by job description.**

_____

_____

_____

_____

_____

_____

_____

Now think of who you want to target in those job descriptions, within your domain.

For example, if you're a financial advisor, you manage other people's money so they don't have to. Your list may include Box 2 people who are your future connections; people who could refer you to future or potential Box 1 connections. These Box 2 people could be decision makers such as accountants, attorneys, bankers, and insurance agents. Or they could be part of a club or association where you could connect with a large group of people who might be Box 1 people. I like to think of it as, "Where in the universe do people need my brand?"

You might target a certain size of business, people within a certain age range, or people in a particular situation, such as people who are just starting a family, use Android phones, or are buying a new home.

For people who are Low Influence/High Familiarity — Box 3 — they have something in common with you but aren't likely to be clients or refer clients to you. These people are highly familiar with you, but you don't expect them to drive business to you. You likely connect with them for reasons other than business, such as belonging to the same golf or hiking group, having kids on the same sports team, or being their dental patient.

People who are Low Influence/Low Familiarity — Box 4 — you don't know well, and you also don't see them influencing your market. These people could be your barista, your bank security guard, or the nurse who gives you a flu shot.

Often, I see people networking with people from the wrong boxes. You'll need to focus your energy into Boxes 1 and 2 if you want to develop more referrals and business. Save Boxes 3 and 4 for casual conversations that don't drive new business.

> ### CASE STUDY: Shifting your focus to clients who value what you offer
>
> I had a client who targeted large "family office" groups as his clients. These family offices are usually created by very wealthy families to manage their money and assets, and they typically have numerous advisors and consultants. As a result, his clients treated him as nothing special — just another commodity service provider among many.
>
> My client realized he didn't really like working with family offices. The families were difficult at best, and unpleasant or even surly at their worst. So he started targeting clients that he would enjoy working with, who wanted what he uniquely offered: clarity.
>
> The problem was that his family office clients all thought they had their own clarity and so they didn't value his offer. They just wanted returns and performance. So they treated him like he was just some low-level staff person whom they could criticize and get upset with. Even when he was doing fantastic work, they criticized him.
>
> So he shifted his business to focus on people who truly valued his offer and said, "Yes, I want clarity." His business expanded rapidly and his stress evaporated. He didn't need to change careers or move to another state, he just shifted who he targeted with his offer. By understanding and communicating his personal brand to different prospects, he was able to shift his business to better clients.

This is also an example of shifting clients from Box 2 to Box 1 and generating new business.

Putting it all together

Now that you have some named contacts to target, you're no doubt very excited to start reaching out and putting your brand to work. But wait! There's more!

As an example, from my personal brand in Chapter 4, I realized that I "create space for people to take it to the next level." My target audience is top-tier professionals and corporate executives who have a sense of urgency about their careers and want new tools and perspectives to get them to their next level. These were my Box 1 and Box 2 targets.

EXERCISE 7.14: What's your offer again?

Write down your offer to your target audience — yes, this is a recap of work you've done in Chapters 4, 5 and 6. Make sure it addresses their specific needs. Your offer might sound like, "I can solve this problem for you by X date," or, "I will show how I can find a better way to solve the problem you're facing now."

This might feel like the commercial you've already done in previous chapters. The difference now is that we're turning this into a conversation starter and door opener with your specific target audience in mind, and in a way that complements your brand.

You must be honest with yourself in this. If your current boss, clients, or coworkers don't want your offer, you might need to find someone who does. If no one wants your offer, then maybe you need to refine it and rethink how to make it valuable.

EXERCISE 7.15: Refining your offer

Reflect back on your offer in the prior exercise. **Can you rephrase the last exercise to use the same terms or phrases that your target audience would use?** Is there any specific industry language you can use to demonstrate you understand their needs and can help solve their problems? I'll bet there is.

Whether you're in real estate, healthcare, law, tech or finance, there are dozens of "terms of art" specific to that industry that subtly communicate your expertise, or that you're an insider.

As you refine your offer and rephrase it, you should also ask yourself: How does my personal brand grow the personal brands of other people?

Think about what's in it for them: professionally, personally, and for their company as a whole. This links back to one of our branding rules: You grow your personal brand to the extent you help others grow their personal brands.

_____

_____

_____

_____

_____

_____

_____

The offer and value conversation

There are two types of conversations you are likely to have with customers before they sign up for your product and services. First is the offer or sales conversation, where you describe features and benefits, trying to be as specific as possible for their situation. The sales conversation allows you to make a general offer — you're giving a sales pitch to entice them to buy what you've got, or at least gain interest.

The second conversation is about value and how you'll meet their needs. Unlike a sales pitch, it's a back-and-forth where you'll seek to discover what your customer values and even why they value these things. Through your questions, you'll help the prospect identify what they would get out of your services and quantify its impact on their life.

The second, more consultative, conversation is much more effective than the first sales pitch. That's because you're offering more specific and personalized value than a sales pitch could, you're helping the customer to realize on their own the benefits of your product or service, and you're establishing how they value it.

This requires questions, research and interest from you. Say a client says we need to set up new systems that will help us track our customers and increase their level of satisfaction and generate repeat business. The next question from you to them should be, "And if you do that, what will that mean in revenue/growth/savings to your business?"

At that point, people can predict what the value is and you will not only understand the magnitude of their situation, but you'll be able to determine if your brand offer can meet their needs.

CASE STUDY: Don't assume what matters most to the client

My colleague recently had a major flood in her house that did nearly $50,000 damage. To fix it, she had to hire a contractor for reconstruction services, and she interviewed seven different contractors to secure bids for the loss that would be covered by insurance.

Some of the contractors came in and immediately started measuring the damaged rooms: how much new carpet, tile, drywall and paint would be needed? Some put together complicated estimates that she couldn't easily understand, so she wasn't sure what the charges were for. Some put together very generalized estimates with a final number — say, $52,314.19 — without any rationale for that amount. The contractors behind both of these kinds of bids assumed she was focusing on one thing: price.

But the contractor who won her business took the time to learn that she was more concerned about speed (having her house put back together after the flood) than price, and more concerned with doing a top-notch job in her custom home than paying out of pocket for higher-grade materials. The contractor that won her business focused on a consultative approach to selling, and their offer lined up perfectly with her wants and needs, which weren't the same as other price-driven customers.

The power of your stories

Being able to tell a story about how you've created success for someone specific in your target market is an essential part of this value conversation. Here are the core components you'll need for your story:

- Link some attributes of the listener to the person the story is about — such as having a similar problem, being in a similar industry, or needing a similar result.
- Talk about the customer's problem in a way that's meaningful to the listener. You might describe the impact of the problem, its size, or a ticking clock.
- Describe how you implemented both your specialized skills *and your approach* to help solve the problem.
- Describe the results in context. Don't just say you saved $100,000 — put it in perspective to explain the significance of this result.

EXERCISE 7.16: What's your story?

Write out a few examples of your stories. Think of specific instances where both your skills and approach were used to help the client get a great result, and be sure to put that result in context.

The customer: _____

_____

The problem: _____

_____

Your skills and approach: _____

_____

Results and context: _____

_____

_____

The customer: _____

_____

The problem: _____

_____

Your skills and approach: _____

_____

Results and context: _____

_____

_____

The customer: _____

_____

The problem: _____

_____

Your skills and approach: _____

_____

Results and context: _____

_____

_____

My example:

A large commercial real estate firm wanted to expand its business in a US region to work with more institutions. They promoted me to lead this effort because of my experience in working with insitutions in the past, and my approach of taking business to the next level.

In five years, I led the region to increase its business from virtually no institutional deals — just $300 million in listings — to more than $5 billion in listings. This established my firm as a true institutional player.

Conclusion

As we talked about in Chapter 3, there are three main methods to getting your message out there.

- Direct selling
- Referrals
- Marketing

The problem with direct selling is that you have to be in the room with them. And for referrals, the person has to have done work with you and be a proud wearer of your "badge of trust" and be willing to refer you to others. Marketing gets your brand message to your target audience without you having to talk to them directly. It's the least time-consuming method of getting your message out there. But it can be costly if you're not using all the tools in this book, because your unique message won't be heard by your target audience.

To summarize, you need to know what your message is, who your target audience is, how to reach them and why your Atomic Brand will benefit them. So make sure you have your commercial or conversation starter ready. Practice it often with family and friends, so that they can remember it and bring you up to their friends, clients, colleagues and acquaintances. That practice will also help you be more confident when you use your conversation starter with a stranger.

We're not quite done here yet. There are still more pieces to this puzzle. When you share your personal commercial, you need to connect with the listener in a way that generates active engagement. That's what the three remaining elements of client discovery are, and what we'll dive into in the following chapters.

But to end this chapter, take a moment to review.

- Do you understand who your current target audience is? Remember that they can be anyone — coworkers, customers, bosses, potential employers, even your cycle class instructor.
- Does your family know your approach?
- Who do you know who can help you reach your target audience?
- What is the main domain that your target audience operates in?
- What is your offer to them?
- How does your offer help grow the brand of your target audience?

Now let's move on to the next chapter and focus on the next branch of your "client discovery tree."

CHAPTER 8
Making empathy part of your process

Objectives

By now you've got a clear idea of your personal brand and who you want to direct it toward. This chapter will focus on how to emotionally connect with your target audience. By the end of this chapter you will understand two things:

- Why demonstrating empathy is important in order for your brand to reach your target audience, and
- How to use empathy to emotionally engage with your target audience.

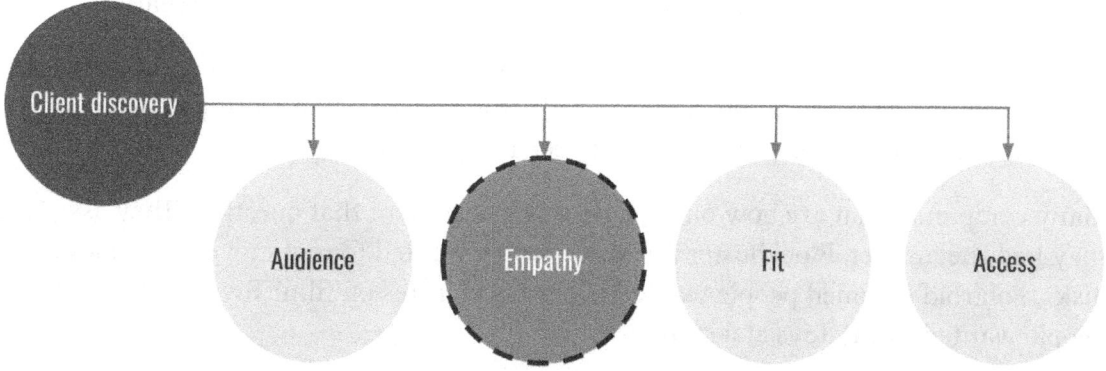

What is empathy?

Empathy is your ability to understand and emotionally connect with your customers' needs.

An easy way to think about empathy is by imagining standing in someone else's shoes — your client, colleague or customer. You can't stand in two pairs of shoes at the same time, so you must get out of your shoes and into theirs.

What do they want and need? How can you help them get it? This is not sympathy, where you look at them from your own perspective and feel sorry for them. This is empathy, where you can see, feel and understand their unique point of view. Empathy is a vital tool for deciding how to adapt your personal brand.

One of the key traits of empathetic people (and one most admired by others) is "being a good listener." As humans, we like to be heard and understood by the people we're engaging with. It's universal. Whether personally or professionally, being heard makes us feel special. Good listening and understanding is an essential way to demonstrate that you care about their needs.

Good listening brings you one of the greatest strengths you can have: clarity. To see things clearly is a huge competitive advantage. Most people see things with their own bias, wants, needs and filters. Being a good listener shows that you're looking for opportunities to help people. But if you're too pushy or intrusive, it can make you off-putting and seem like you have what we call in the business, "commission breath."

True empathy is understanding what is going on for your target audience. To drive this home, I ask people to answer this for me: "What is needed?" The more you listen and understand, the clearer you will be able to see the answer.

Many companies that are now out of business lost sight of that question. They assumed they had the answer. Blockbuster assumed people wanted to rent movies on tapes or disks. Polaroid assumed people wanted to record pictures on film. Toys "R" Us assumed people wanted to buy toys at a store.

Many small businesses focus their efforts on a statement like this: "I need more work, so I can pay bills ASAP." At an employee level, a person might say, "I want to collect a paycheck, but I need to get out of this life-sucking company. I really hate my job."

These didn't demonstrate empathy for their target audience. By listening carefully to what the customer says, and by observing their subtle actions, you'll learn exactly what your target audience needs and precisely how your brand can get them there. This will differentiate you from your competitors.

How to use and practice empathy

Some people are born with natural empathy. Some of us have to learn and practice it. Practicing empathy is about focusing on someone else's needs instead of your own. In relationships, it might mean showing your partner they're loved by bringing them coffee in the morning or sending your mother flowers — not just on Mother's Day, and exactly the kind you know she likes.

In the business world, it can be harder to determine. Here are a few starting points to help you identify it:

- What does your target business/person care about?
- What are their immediate priorities?
- If they're a new software company, is their focus developing a more stable platform? Building their subscriber base?
- If they're in real estate, are they trying to construct a new building or renovate an existing one? Are they looking for investors or buyers or tenants?
- If they're a product, are they looking to sell more units per buyer, sell to buyers more frequently, or expand their pool of buyers?

Next, ask: What are they trying to accomplish that makes you relevant to their needs? If it's the software company, perhaps your expertise is building loyal audiences and customer engagement. In real estate, maybe you can make introductions to potential investors, or you can advise them on structuring a lease.

Third, consider how they make decisions. Does the CEO make decisions solo, or with input from the executive team or the board of directors? Is your target customer a small business with one frazzled and impulsive owner? Will your proposal go through a detailed procurement process, or will the risk-averse department manager want to know every possible outcome? Or, perhaps, are they big-picture people who just want concise bullet points and references? All of these ideas can apply to a potential new prospect or employer.

You need to know this decision-making process because if you submit a proposal to a detail-oriented client that only offers high-level bullet points, it won't address their key concerns. Even if you're the best person for the job, you've already lost.

> ### CASE STUDY: Over-deliver for the person, not just the business
>
> We had a large client that was very concerned with high-quality reporting on the investments he controlled. We went way over the top to help him deliver on those reports.
>
> One day, he complained about not getting Barney (the dinosaur) tickets for his son because they had sold out in 10 minutes. We got him front-row seats to the show.
>
> It was a small gesture, but as a result, he gave us a fantastic amount of business. That was next-level stuff. All we did was say, "What is the next level for us with this client?" And surprisingly, it wasn't just the reports.

Overcoming the language barrier

Yes, there's a main language that's spoken depending on the country you're in: English, Spanish, Japanese, etc. But there's also the technical language of your industry.

In law, these words are often called "terms of art." And in any industry, there are terms and vernacular used exclusively by people in that industry. To demonstrate your understanding of your target audience's specific needs, you need to translate your offer into their industry language and transcend this language barrier.

It's important to start by using the right terms. In real estate investing, it would be terms like, "IRR," that is, the internal rate of return on an investment, or "loan amortization." In the tech world, you might talk about specific programming languages such as Python, Java, or C++.

> **When talking about your brand, you need to be able to share your offer in terms your target audience will understand.**

If I'm talking to a runner, they understand "hard day and recovery day." If I'm talking to a lawyer, they understand the terms "rainmaker" or "litigant" in a particular way.

Sometimes the expert gets too caught up in their own area of expertise. For example, the leader of a marketing agency might be pitching to a small business owner. If they use terms like "CPC" (cost per click) and "bounce rate" without context, they could risk alienating the small business owner who wants the marketing agency to bring clients into her dental practice. The marketing agency leader needs to adapt their language to reflect the dentist's terminology, such as attracting new "patients" rather than "customers."

As another example, if you're developing a brand as a website designer with a point-of-sale focus, you need to be able to talk about the marketing funnel, cart abandonment rates and total cart values. You need to show how you'll achieve a higher transaction completion rate. Demonstrating your knowledge isn't about throwing out marketing jargon; what counts is whether you can directly link your skills and track record to their specific needs. Making that link goes back to empathy and building a relationship to uncover those needs.

If you're not sure about the language specifics, it never hurts to do research. Read articles in their industry magazines. You don't even need to attend a trade show to get a sense of what professionals in that industry are currently wrestling with or debating. Instead, check out the trade show's website where featured speakers' abstracts are often posted (better yet, some are recorded and shared on YouTube and other platforms).

The more you can demonstrate your understanding/empathy the better. There's no such thing as being over-prepared!

I realize that if you are new to an industry, you might not know its specific language. When I started my career in commercial real estate in my early twenties, it was like a foreign language. My manager hired me because I knew how to turn on a computer and use it for financial analysis — which was rare at the time. If you don't know the industry lingo yet, you need to show them other strengths that can benefit them.

Let's say you're interested in working for an organic food manufacturer. You don't know the industry lingo, but perhaps you have social media skills to promote the brand, or you can lean into your college DJ promotions experience to host on-site tastings or distribution at events.

You can dig into the catalog of experiences and skills you've already written down to find a way to use your unique approach for their benefit. Your task is to make the connection clear.

EXERCISE 8.1: Using their language

Look at your contact list from Chapter 7 and **answer these questions:**

What needs do they have? _____

_____

_____

_____

How can you demonstrate that you understand and can help them?

_____

_____

_____

What language or terms are specific to their industry? _____

_____

_____

_____

How does your personal brand get them the solution they are looking for?

_____

_____

_____

Conclusion

This was a short and sweet chapter, but it asks you to spend some time on reflection. Don't just assume what your customers want and need. Use empathy in your business to better uncover what they desire.

Before you move on...

The most important thing you can do in business is see what's needed. Empathy is one of the key tools to help you reveal that need. In the coming week, fine-tune your listening and observation skills of empathy in action.

- Does customer service anticipate your needs, or do you have to explain everything to them?
- What about a server in a restaurant?
- What about your dentist or financial planner?
- Where are you seeing empathy in action?

This can be hard to observe because your transaction with them will feel effortless. But that's exactly what you want to build for your own clients.

CHAPTER 9
Finding the perfect fit

Objectives

In this chapter, you'll learn:

- Why it's important to find the right client — not just any client.
- How to find a company whose brand complements yours.

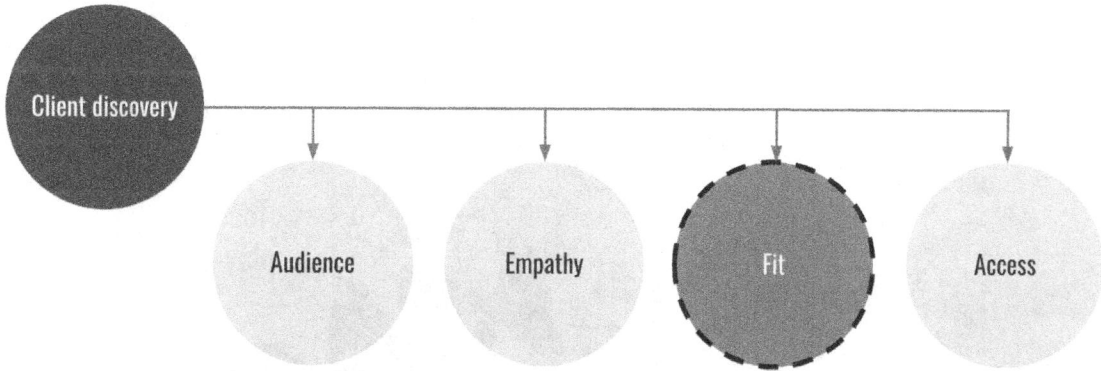

The right fit for you

Earlier, we talked about being pigeonholed and how that can make you miserable. Likewise, you might be in the right job or working with the right type of client, but still experiencing a major personality clash. In either case, the ultimate result is damage to your personal brand … and this clash can also damage your self-esteem, health (from stress), and overall happiness.

We've been taught from an early age how to "fit in" — not how to find the place we fit. Essentially, that's what this book is all about: Finding out who you are, what your unique approach and skills are, so you can find the right people and career.

If you're using your personal brand to land yourself in a company, then it's important to know what other skill sets or personal brands would complement yours. If your brand is clear, people will be able to decide quickly whether and how to work with you. And if their brand is clear, you'll make more informed decisions about who you want to work with.

See an example below. Each of these people have a unique set of skills that complement each other.

Your personal brand should be linked to the team brand and enhance it. And that team brand should support the larger company or divisional brand.

Let's say you're the efficient person on your team. You should be able to show your senior team leader how that helps the team brand. And the team should be able to show how they, in turn, support the company brand.

The problem comes up when either your brand doesn't fit with the team, or your brand is too abstract to clearly define.

The diagram below is a visual representation of what we've discussed in previous chapters.

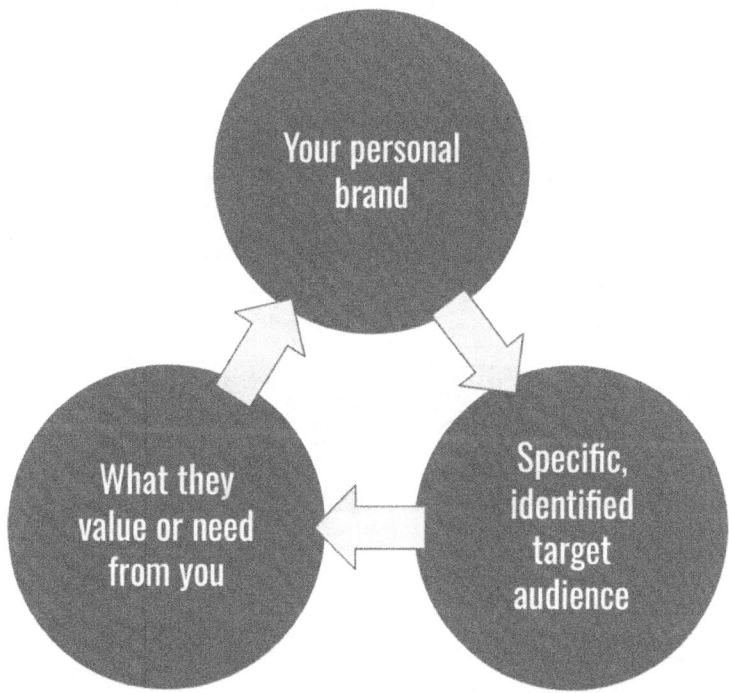

Let's apply this to working within a corporate culture. In my case, it would have been hard to position myself in a company as the "Robbins Brand" or the "Blue Team" brand, because that doesn't mean anything to the division or the company as whole.

Your brand must give your team, the company, and your clients value. Your job is to look for where they want value and figure out how you can deliver increased value in the future. As per the diagram below:

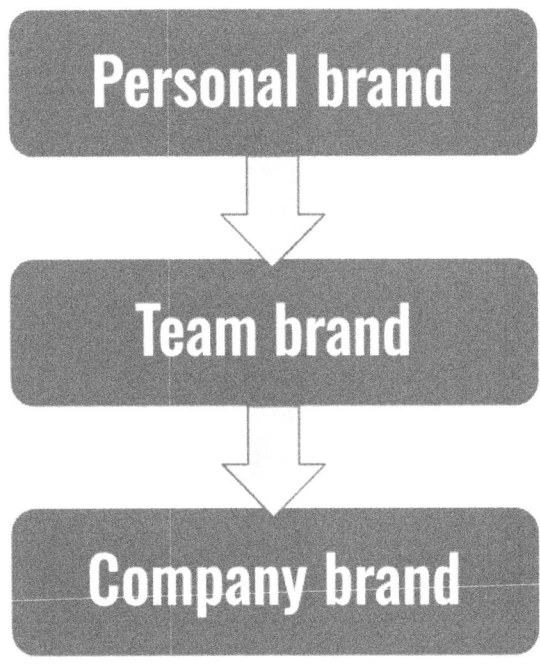

EXERCISE 9.1: How your brand fits in

Identify your top assets that are most distinctive and relevant to your target audience — in this case, to your team or company.

Refer back to your inventory list. What we're doing now is taking your inventory to the next level. We're going to apply it to determine what corporate culture or team would be a good fit for you.

_____   _____

_____   _____

_____   _____

_____   _____

_____   _____

_____   _____

_____   _____

_____   _____

_____   _____

Here's my list from when I was in a global corporate position, before I became a performance coach:

- 20+ years in real estate
- Deep innovative business expertise
- Loopnet
- Created Colliers University
- CKO Global Company
- Passionate
- World traveler cultural awareness
- Expertise on personal branding

- Strong interest in others' growth
- Experienced public speaker
- Very well informed on current events
- Excellent instincts with clients
- First-rate people skills
- Motivator
- Thinker
- Curious about innovations

EXERCISE 9.2: What's your theme?

Now group your assets by key themes, such as in my example below:

INVENTORY	THEME
Thinker Curious about innovations Worn many hats in real estate	Curious
Motivator Passionate Enthusiastic	Mood builder
20+ years in real estate Deep business experience/ systems Identity and branding expert	Expertise
Interest in others Client instincts People skills, world traveled	Integrator
Started Colliers University Started Loopnet Chief Knowledge Officer	Vision

This is another side of the work you've done, where we looked at how your brand can benefit your audience. Sometimes coming at things from a slightly different angle can help you define your approach.

Your turn here: **Pick your dominant themes** based on what you know about your target audience.

INVENTORY	THEME
	)
	)
	)
	)
	)

This is another side of the work you've done, where we looked at how your brand can benefit your audience. Sometimes coming at things from a slightly different angle can help you define your approach.

EXERCISE 9.3: Finessing the fit

Let's take a quick look at your fit from another angle. Reviewing your inventory and attributes from previous exercises, **what are some skills and approaches that would complement yours?**

For example:

- If you're very analytical, what might complement you is a great salesperson.
- If you're great at building teams and getting everyone to work together, what might complement you is a strategic thinker.
- You might be great a minimizing risk, but you need someone who can make decisions that might include risk.
- You might be excellent at generating an action plan, but you need someone creative on your team to help you think outside the box.

Essentially, you're looking for capabilities and approaches that are the yin to your yang, or people who have strengths in areas where your skills are less developed.

On the left, write down your strengths and weaknesses. Then, on the right, write down skills or attributes from other people that would complement yours.

YOUR ATTRIBUTES	COMPLEMENTARY FIT

EXERCISE 9.4: Where do you want to fit?

Okay, so now you know what your skills are and what approach you have to offer that would complement others. But here's the really important question: **Where do you want to fit?** Be thoughtful about where you want to apply your brand.

_____

_____

_____

_____

_____

_____

> ### CASE STUDY: Does your audience really want your offer?
>
> I took a job where the CEO said he really wanted me to deliver next-level coaching to a department. The money was really good, but as I began the training, I quickly realized that the CEO didn't want to go through the coaching and just wanted me to fix his slow-moving leadership team.
>
> Worse, the leadership team already felt they were on the right track and didn't want to improve. In short, neither the CEO nor the team wanted to go to the next level. I swore I would never work for a company that didn't value my brand again. I also swore I wouldn't work with a group of people that didn't have a strong hand in hiring me in the first place.
>
> Now, when a boss calls me and asks me to coach their team, I ask if the team has asked for it. If the answer is no, my radar goes up. Most companies implement unrequested training for all kinds of reasons. Maybe HR wants points on the board, or the division leader is not happy with performance. All of this causes anxiety, resentment and resignation for the team. If the team isn't aware enough to want coaching, or doesn't think they need it, it's not a good fit for me (or for them).

Yes, financial security is important. You want to build a business that supports your lifestyle. But it's never worth it at the expense of your health or happiness. Don't just do it for the money. Playing out of position and just tolerating your job degrades your quality of life.

This is the biggest mistake good people make in their careers. Ask yourself: Would you fit into an office environment where you're required to show up at 9 a.m. sharp, no matter what? Or would you rather work on flexible hours?

Do you work better around other people or by yourself? Are you goal-oriented? Do you prefer to be self-accountable or check in with a team? Would you rather be in a job where you react (they come to you) or proactive (you get new things going)?

Remember fit goes in both directions. Your career should fit your work style and lifestyle choices — even if those come with a trade-off with other things that matter to you less.

Would you take a 20% pay cut to work a four-day week? That suggests you're willing to trade making more money for having more free time. Would you be willing to "fire" a high-paying customer if they are rude and abusive? That suggests you're willing to make less money in exchange for kindness and peace of mind. Think about whether your clients and their expectations are a good fit for you (or vice versa).

EXERCISE 9.5: Finding where you want to fit

Answer as many of the following questions as you can.

Whom do you want to be accountable to?

What do you want to be responsible for?

What kinds of decisions do you want to be able to make?

What kinds of relationships do you want? (boss, coworkers, clients)

How do you want to be treated?

What core values do you want to be associated with?

What pace do you want?

What reputation by association do you want?

What physical environment do you want?

What compensation and benefits do you want or need?

Sure, your next client or job may not offer all of these things, but if your core needs and values are being met, along with their core values and needs — it's a win-win.

I actually did this after I had fully discovered and embraced my personal brand. I wrote out each of these questions and answers to establish a future vision for myself. It helped me determine where I would be a good fit.

CASE STUDY: Defining your target

One of my former colleagues was recruited by her former boss to join a "dream team" — a new marketing department in a recently reorganized company.

In a previous company, they'd worked together flawlessly, but in the new role, the relationship soured. It turned out the reorganized company was floundering, and that pressure was rolling downhill, from the board, to firing the CEO, to the very real possibility that her boss, the CMO, would also be fired.

Instead of a great collaborator, her boss became a tyrant. She knew she had to move on, but she didn't want to "jump out of the frying pan and into the fire" with another unknown company that could potentially be just as bad.

So she took stock of all of the roles and companies she'd worked for previously, making notes on what she enjoyed and what motivated her. She liked working flexibly across many projects, supervising and growing a team, working in an international company, working with a small startup, and working with "martech," which is technology created specifically for marketers.

That sounds too specific — how could she find a small, international martech company? She researched more than 50 tech companies founded outside the U.S. but growing their North American presence, and finally joined a martech startup as employee No. 120 (among the first 15 Americans hired). That diligent research paid off in landing a leadership role at a high-growth company with a new boss who she could call collaborator, mentor and friend.

Conclusion

Now you should have a clear idea of where you fit and what's a good fit for you. You can also use empathy and your brand to better understand your target audience and find the right fit. See? It's all working together.

Once you figure out your personal brand, you'll want to use every tool you can to amplify and reinforce it. For example, you can go on Google and search your personal brand to find other brands to connect with it. If you're all about fast, you might dive deep into Ferrari's branding for inspiration. Or if you're about precision, take cues from a high-end watch brand. My "next level" brand means I need to show clients how I take everything I can to the next level … and if you ever eat my homemade pizza, you'll agree even that is "next level."

Before you move on...

AI is a fantastic tool to help you start researching your own brand. Also consider Google Image Search, or trends.google.com, which can reveal how keywords in your industry are popular over time. Look at answerthepublic.com, which shows both keywords and the long-form questions people are asking Google about that subject.

Consider asking bard.google.com, "What does it mean to be a [insert your Atomic Brand] in [insert your industry]?" You'll find it spins up a multitude of examples. Make your research notes here:

_____

_____

_____

_____

_____

_____

_____

_____

_____

_____

_____

_____

_____

CHAPTER 10
Access and action

Objectives

By now you know who your dream clients (target audience) are. You know who you want to reach and how to use empathy to show you can meet their needs. First, we're going to look at one thing, and one thing only: How to access your target audience.

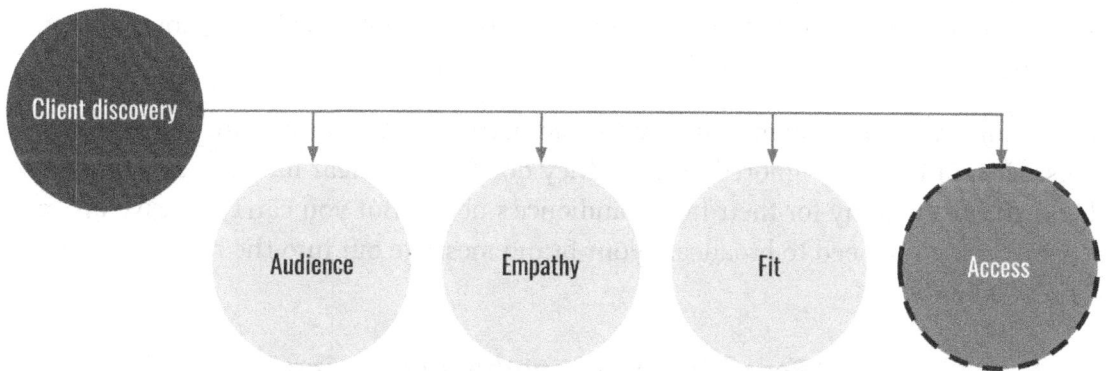

Then we'll put it into practice — ensuring you deliver your Atomic Brand to your intended market. By the end of this chapter you'll understand:

- How to put your business plan into concrete action.
- How to ensure you deliver on your promises.
- How to use client feedback to improve your services.
- How you can keep using increased business to improve your services.

Once you're finished, you'll have everything you'll need to be your own personal branding powerhouse. And the best thing about it? It will perfectly align with your authentic self and unique attributes, and your target audience's desires.

Access your target audience

You know who your dream/potential companies, employers, industry or clients are. You know you can empathize with their needs and help solve their problems. You have a good idea on who and what would be a good fit for you. That leaves one main question ... how?

As we mentioned earlier, there are three main methods:

- **Direct selling** — in person/face to face/talking
- **Referrals** — get someone to tell someone else about you (also known as "pre-sold")
- **Marketing** — making your brand offer without talking to somebody

Since this book is about using your brand to market yourself, we're going to focus on No. 3. I worked with a real estate broker who decided to send his prospects $50 for a 30-minute meeting with him (this was in the late 1980s). He got a big group of people to respond, and it gave him the attention he needed to make his brand offer.

The trouble with marketing is that nobody likes being sold to. But people do like getting value. The issue is that the perception of value lies with the buyer, not with you, the seller. Value is a buyer's word — not a seller's word.

We're constantly being bombarded with cold-marketing emails and unwanted phone calls. Most of these get ignored because they don't have a clear message and they don't demonstrate empathy for their target audience's needs. But you can't just give up on reaching out. You need to broadcast your brand message out into the market of your target audience.

> **"Repetition in the mother of learning."**
> **— Zig Zigler**

It has been my experience that your audience needs to hear it eight times before they start to remember you. So while you don't want to waste money on marketing, you need a plan for getting your message across.

Assuming you have...

- A clear message
- Demonstrated empathy for their needs
- Shown or offered value

... how do you then access your clients? Here are just a few ideas to get you started:

ACCESS: In person

- Client events
- Networking events
- Trade & other memberships
- Seminars
- Door knocking — walking the market
- Nonprofit involvement
- Volunteering

ACCESS: By phone

- Cold calls
- Warm calls
- Referral calls

ACCESS: In print

- Direct mail
- Ads & brochures
- Signage
- Articles
- Newsletters

ACCESS: Digital

- Websites — YouTube, Reddit, Quora, etc.
- Online ads
- Email
- Articles
- Blogs
- Webinars
- Podcasts
- Newsletters

ACCESS: Social media

- Facebook
- X (formerly Twitter)
- Instagram
- TikTok
- Snapchat
- Clubhouse
- Triberr
- LinkedIn

Remember, all you are trying to do is to put your brand offer in front of your target audience. They will then decide if it's of value to them.

I ask people this question, "If I gave you a pill to sell that made people live to 100 years old with no diseases, do you think it would be easy to get meetings to tell people about it? Do you think everyone would buy it?" Invariably, a huge number of people wouldn't buy it — from the anti-pharma crowd to the people who don't want to give up their sick days.

Building a brand is about realizing you're making an offer to people about you, your approach and skills, so they can decide if they want it. The reality of branding is that most people don't understand how to make their offer to others and frame it as a selfish benefit.

EXERCISE 10.1: Reaching your target audience

Refer to your contact list. What do you think your target audience uses most often to connect and communicate? Depending on their age and other demographics, the answer is likely to vary widely.

List these communication channels below. Remember: The point is not to hassle or stalk. The goal is to engage in conversation. Attraction via promotion. Mickey Mouse doesn't follow you home from Disneyland!

Your action plan components

Now we have all of the pieces of client discovery! So far, you've identified your:

- Target audience (market or client)
- Access points
- Marketing plan

You understand who you're trying to target, how to connect with them emotionally, how to determine if they're the right fit for you and how to access them. This is essentially your business plan. Next, let's put it into action.

A brand would be nothing if it didn't have action. Disney wouldn't exist if it didn't have Disney movies, theme parks and deliver on its promise to provide your entire family with feel-good, heartwarming entertainment.

The final element is how to effectively use your access once you have it. How to turn your plan into action. You should already have an answer to these questions:

- What do you want to be known for?
- Who should know about you?
- How are you going to deliver your message?

You've already done the hard work here. The exercises in Chapter 4 created your 30-second commercial. So the big question is, now what?

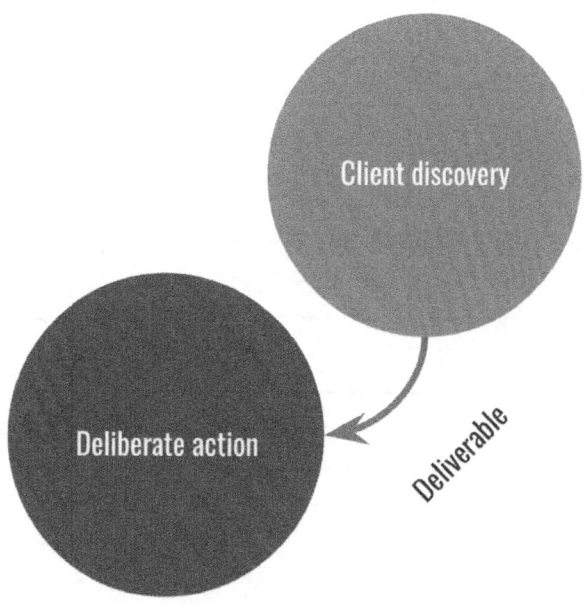

Own the next step

Typically, I've found that the people who control the deal own the next step in the process. They know what they want to happen next, and they know how to steer their audience in that direction to get a mutually beneficial outcome.

If you can't own the next step, at least know how to ask for it. Let's say you've taken your brand offer to a potential client, and they're interested. What steps do you want to have happen next? Here are some possible examples:

- Ask for the sale or meeting — contracts signed

- Be a connector — offer to introduce them to someone

- "Would you like to get together to see how we can help one another develop more business?"

- Wait and see — just say thanks for considering me or meeting with me, and do nothing until they contact you. It might not be appropriate to talk about your brand at that moment. Instead, you might be just listening and demonstrating you understand their needs and are excited to be there.

EXERCISE 10.2: Your action steps

You've made your offer. **What do you want to happen next?** How will you ask for that?

Follow through, follow up, level up

This can't be emphasized enough: Follow up! Follow up! Follow up! If you're playing hard to get, give it a week or two before reaching out. Have your follow-up question ready. Ask or follow up with something you discussed in the last meeting.

Did they get their project approved? Perhaps they had a small business problem, and you have a solution that might be helpful.

Remember to use your empathy and demonstrate understanding of their needs — but also read the room. You don't want to come off as pushy.

The value conversation

Assuming that you nail your brand, and you get that meeting, sales pitch, interview or career discussion with your employer, what next? It's useful to have your commercialized approach (from exercises 4.7 and 4.8 in Chapter 4) ready to use.

Or, if you've already used it to get in the room, you need to be ready to add more detail and value. Alternatively, you might reiterate your brand in a more conversational manner.

Your value conversation should have the following elements:

- **Introduction**: This can include your name, company name, what you do — not just technical skills, but also your approach, the problems you solve, etc. — and who you do it for.

- **An example/testimonial**: Describe how you solved a similar problem for someone else, or some great results you had for a similar client. The key to a good example is to anchor it either to the problem, the customer, or both.

- You might start with, "I noticed that you have a similar problem to my client X..." and then speak to the similarities of these problems. Another hook could be, "I noticed you are in the same industry, or have a similar business model, to my client X" and then explain the similarities between your existing happy client and the prospective client in front of you.

- **Action Steps**: What you want the next step to be — do you want them to introduce you to other people? Review a proposal? Make a specific business decision that moves the sales conversation forward? Or agree to take a meeting and talk more later on?

EXERCISE 10.3: Your value conversation basics

Fill in the blanks below. This should be easy by now — you have these answers at your fingertips! Notice that I haven't given you much writing space here. That's deliberate — you want to be as succinct as possible. Remember your target audience's time is valuable.

- What is your technical skill?

_____

- What is your unique approach?

_____

- Who are you trying to focus on?

_____

- What are their needs?

_____

- Craft an offer that your target audience will respond to:

_____

_____

_____

- What is a short testimonial that supports the above?

_____

_____

_____

EXERCISE 10.4: More of your value conversation

Next, create your own value conversation. This isn't a script, this is a guideline. It is a dialogue between two people — not a monologue where you do all the talking.

The concept here is to walk into your meeting being as prepared as possible. This means knowing who you're talking to, how you can help them, what the ideal outcome would be for both parties and what you want to happen next.

As in any conversation, you need to be able to demonstrate your empathy, ability to listen, and understanding of their needs. If things go off plan, be flexible and gently steer back where appropriate.

My example: You know how so many people feel like they're not advancing fast enough in their companies? Like, they need new ideas? I solve that with a set of counterintuitive tools designed to accelerate their career growth. From finding a new career, to building a company or team, to increasing their number of clients. My clients report a 40% to 400% growth rate in their business after implementing my systems — and most of the time, they say they accomplished this in fewer hours.

What's your value conversation? Again, you haven't got much room here. That's deliberate. Less is more!

_____

_____

_____

You already know what actions and outcomes you want from this value conversation. And let's assume you nailed it — now you've got a new client.

Is your work here done? No. Why not? Because now your brand depends on...

Delivering on the brand promise

This is where most entrepreneurs and ambitious business owners fall down: Delivering on their brand promise. It's easy to sell yourself and make promises, but once the business, client or promotion is landed, what if the work doesn't get done in time, or with the quality the customer has been promised?

If you're serious about building your brand and business, this is the moment to get honest with yourself. Are you giving what you promised? Or, now that you've landed their business, are you focused on what you can get from the transaction?

If you're not meeting your audience's needs, be it for a client or employer, not only are you jeopardizing your relationship with them, but you're jeopardizing your brand as well.

How do you measure whether you are successfully delivering on your brand's promise? There's an entire body of research and several best-selling books devoted to answering this question, such as *The Ultimate Question* by Fred Reichheld.

In that book, the author claims that "satisfaction" is not the end game. Satisfaction is table stakes for delivering on your brand promise, and the ultimate measure of success (hence, the "ultimate question") is whether your customer would actively and enthusiastically refer you to their peers.

Think of defining success in terms of whether your target audience believes they've gotten at least as much value as expected — ideally more — and not just in terms of whether you'll get more future business from them.

Finding your systems

Systems are a set of processes, actions and behaviors
you put in place to achieve a result.

What systems do you have in place to ensure you deliver value? There should be more than one. Brushing your teeth is a system. So is doing payroll, asking for a referral, or managing your work schedule. Asking clients what they value is a system if you have it figured out.

Time management, checklists, onboarding, reporting, and customer care are all systems. Some systems need technology, some need actions, some need other people. Remember to build and use systems to allow your work and business to progress. This should also include asking for feedback from your clients so that you can improve each system over time.

EXERCISE 10.5: Finding your systems

What systems do you have in place to ensure you deliver value? Where do you need help to deliver value? List them. If you don't have any yet, what systems do you need? Start building them.

I have a number of friends who've told me, "I want to be a life coach." The first question I ask them is, "What systems do you have in place to gain or support your potential clients?"

_____

_____

_____

_____

_____

_____

Start, stop, more and less

The next exercise is a quick and easy way to take an inventory of your strengths and weaknesses and adjust your course. Nobody is perfect. Life happens — you might have gotten sick, which impacted your ability to work. You are human. This chart will help you identify extraneous work circumstances and potentially destructive patterns.

This also provides you with a path forward to adjust your focus. You'll identify areas where you can trim or fully stop activities, so you'll have more room to do things that amplify your brand or deliver greater value.

Strategic neglect

It is OK to decide not to do some kinds of work. Call it strategic or systematic neglect. "I don't do that" is not a bad thing. Saying no to certain work can free you to focus on and accept more of the work you prefer to do.

McDonald's doesn't sell pizza in most markets. They probably lose a lot of business from pizza-lovers. But a narrow menu is a core part of McDonald's success, because that focus enabled the company to accelerate the speed of fulfilling orders.

Is the work you want to decline part of your brand promise? For example, if your brand promise is "deep, personal attention," then you can't just assign an assistant to reply to client correspondence, because you've promised to do that personally. But you could have an assistant handle everything else, such as vendors and administration.

If you want to strategically neglect work that's part of your brand promise, now is the time to go back and revise your offer to the market.

But maybe the work you'd rather not do isn't a core part of your brand promise. Good news: You've got options.

- You could revise your scope of services.
- You could outsource this component of your work.
- You could partner with or hire someone who loves to do this work.

If you have unintentionally neglected some areas of your business, this is an opportunity for you to acknowledge that, adjust course and continue to grow.

Serving clients outside of your target market

Some people will ask whether they should continue to do business that might be a bit outside of their target market, or provide services that are not quite within their brand promise. For example, you might have a client who has been loyal for a long time, although your ideal customer is different from them now. Should you dump them?

I advise people to ensure that at least 80% of their focus is on their target market, and then 20% of your time can be spent on those outside of your target — such as longtime customers, those who you are passionate about helping, or "experiments" into areas where you would like to grow your business.

EXERCISE 10.6: Self-evaluation and reflection

Create your own lists within the framework supplied on the following pages. You'll ask yourself:

- What actions and activities are inconsistent with your brand?
- What actions and activities best align?
- What actions can you take today to better align your brand?

We're carving out new time for you by identifying activities you should end or decrease. Then, with these actions eliminated, you have created the space to build new habits, systems or projects.

This framework was introduced with the principles of agile project management, with authors such as Diana Larsen and Esther Derby in their book, *Agile Retrospectives* (2006), and used in another permutation by Michael Gerber in *The E-Myth Revisited* (2009).

STOP: What are you doing that violates your brand or keeps you from doing brand-aligned activities?

_____   _____

_____   _____

_____   _____

LESS: What are you doing now that isn't consistent with your brand?

_____   _____

_____   _____

_____   _____

MORE: What are you doing now that aligns well with your brand?

_____   _____

_____   _____

_____   _____

START: What new things could you be doing that generates or reinforces your brand?

_____   _____

_____   _____

_____   _____

Ongoing validation: Is it working?

Reflection, validation and valuation are essential. Everything changes. Change is the only constant. Ongoing validation will allow you to see if your brand is getting the results you want. Adjust if necessary. It feeds directly into taking deliberate action and allows for strategic growth, leading to better results.

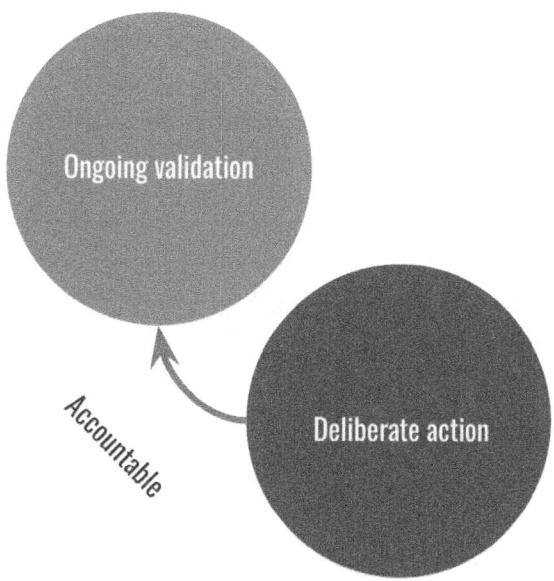

Results

Your ongoing validation will depend on your ability to measure and evaluate your results, so you can continue to adjust your brand or target audience if necessary. There are lots of ways to measure and evaluate results: Google analytics, click monitoring, the number of calls you receive, growth from your email list subscribers, or even asking customers what they know about your brand.

The ultimate goal still remains: Is your brand working? There are three areas to focus on:

- **Brand awareness**: Are you getting the word out? Are they listening? Are they saying your brand back to you?
- **Brand strength**: Are they choosing you? Are they getting what you promised? And are they telling others?
- **Brand stories**: What can you capture and use to reinforce your branding efforts? Do you have a quantifiable (numeric) or qualitative (descriptive) result that you can package in a case study or succinct story? As examples, consider the ones I've given you throughout this book.

Negative feedback isn't actually negative

Many people have a deep fear of negative feedback. They view it as a personal attack. But direct feedback is a useful tool to help you to understand whether you and your brand are delivering the results promised. If you're not, then clearly some adjustment is needed.

For example, if you're having trouble delivering your services within the timeframe you promised, perhaps you need to adjust your timeframe or get more support. Instead of a three- to five-day turnaround, make it 14 days. If you deliver it early, it's a win-win. Managing expectations through effective communication is key to delivering on your brand promise.

Actively seeking feedback from a client on what you can do to improve your services helps you gain their trust. Why? You are demonstrating empathy and humility, which makes them feel listened to. Maybe it won't all be glowing reviews, but it will be things you can learn from to improve your future results.

EXERCISE 10.7: Create a survey

Create a survey, form or series of questions for your current clients for them to give you feedback. Make sure it addresses your main areas of concern and gives them room to give feedback for your improvement. It doesn't need to be detailed. It could just be two or three questions with a rating of 1 to 5 stars.

The key here is to use this as an opportunity to learn and improve. Asking and creating a safe space for constructive dialogue also helps to build trust with your audience and strengthens your relationship.

Feedback shouldn't come just from one source. Coworkers, employees, other divisions, even competitors can be really helpful here. You need to constantly evaluate for yourself to ensure your brand is working and adjust as necessary.

EXERCISE 10.8: Pinpointing areas for improvement

Jot down answers to these. Remember: The point here isn't to beat yourself up. The point is to learn, adapt and improve so you can grow your business.

Are you able to meet your client targets?

Are you meeting your own business targets?

Are you getting the right kind of clients?

Are you getting the results you want?

Are you listening to your clients, and are they listening to you?

Is your 30-second commercial effective?

What needs to happen to better help you and your clients?

What actions can you take to improve your results?

EXERCISE 10.9: What else?

After going through all of these previous exercises in this chapter, do you have any other thoughts or notes on what actions you can take in the future?

Before you skip this step, imagine that you have to come up with three more things. That could be three more actions to start or stop; three more things you could strategically neglect; three more resources you could use to amplify your message.

I've found that challenging myself to add three more things can often uncover the most surprising or profound insights. Set a timer for five minutes and sit with this question. Don't ask, "Anything else?" Instead ask, "What else?" and let your mind generate three more things.

_____

_____

_____

Conclusion

We've come full circle. Congratulations! You now have an Atomic Brand, an audience to target, and a way to continually refine and improve it.

I hope this book has been helpful in taking you and your business or role to the next level. Remember: You can continue to refine and adjust. There's no timetable here except yours.

Do you have a success story? Please share it! I'd love to hear how this book helped you.

Reach out with stories and questions via my website: **CraigRobbinsNextLevel.com**.

I also welcome your feedback — positive and negative. If there's anything you think should be clearer, let me know! I'm always looking for a way to take my services to the next level too.

Before you wrap up...

Let's go back to page 8, where I asked you to jot down notes on what you wanted to accomplish with this book. How will you know you're successful? What specifically do you want to improve in your business?

After reading this book, have your answers changed? Do you have an action plan for what to do next with your business, starting today? What does that look like?

APPENDIX

Quiz Answers

Exercise 2.1

- A: Apple
- B: McDonald's
- C: Tesla
- D: Nike
- E: Louis Vuitton

Exercise 2.2

- A: Red Bull
- B: BMW
- C: L'Oréal
- D: FedEx
- E: Nike

Exercise 2.3

- A: FedEx — fastest, overnight
- B: Farmers Insurance — the smartest insurance company
- C: Chanel — elite, luxury ready-to-wear

GLOSSARY

- **Access**: The opportunity and methods to reach a specific group of people.

- **Action phrase**: Words to describe our differentiated approach as an action.

- **Analyzers**: People who make decisions based on a deep dive into data and history. They are typically focused on prudence, safety, security, accountability and standards.

- **Approach**: (also called core approach) Your baseline perspective or point of view. It's the way you bring yourself to a situation, task, interaction or role.
  See also: commercial approach.

- **Atomic Brand**: Your personal brand, grounded in your perspective, guided by your approach, and deliberately designed to address the needs of your chosen market. Everyone has a personal brand, but not all personal brands are Atomic Brands. What sets Atomic Brands apart is their ability to produce energy, prosperity, and personal and professional satisfaction.

- **Autonomy**: The ability to self-direct and decide on your own course of action in a given situation.

- **Badge**: A way of saying the people you work with — company, boss, coworkers, friends, family, customers or clients — trust you and are willing to tell others.

- **Benefit**: Tangible, valuable outcomes the target audience receives as a result of buying, using or experiencing a product or service.

- **Brand**: A promise, from one party to another, about what they can expect to experience from buying a product or service.

- **Brand equity**: The residual emotional experience someone takes away from an interaction after buying a product or service.

- **Capabilities:** Specific and demonstrable skills we have at our disposal.

- **Commercial approach:** The way we frame our core approach to make it into an offer that people are willing to pay for. *See also: approach.*

- **Credentials:** Experiences, certifications, awards and other accolades that help people decide if we are believable.

- **Credibility:** The qualifications and credentials that make us trusted or believed in.

- **Do-ers:** People who want to get it done. They are in motion, stay in motion, and focus on serving needs.

- **Dominant approach:** The strongest most consistent way we handle situations. The way we think about, act, feel, and focus on situations, and is largely subconscious. Typically, it is consistently observed in both personal life and work. As our primary way of being, it becomes the basis of our personal brand.

- **Domain:** The sphere or area you act in; the realm in which you establish knowledge, skills and expertise. A person can have many domains, such as in work, food, health, fitness, money, etc.

- **Empathy:** Your ability to understand and emotionally connect with your customers' needs.

- **Features:** The attributes, skills, and functions of the product or services you provide.

- **First impression:** What people initially think about you at the first meeting. It is the person's observations, conversation and experience, combined with their pre-existing stereotypes, experiences, knowledge and feelings.

- **Habits:** An ingrained, frequent action that is often done unconsciously, so it becomes mostly unobserved.

- **Identity:** The interpretation, by self or by others, of a person's overall significance. How the market perceives you, your value and your way of being. How you see yourself as being different from others.

- **Intention:** The purpose of an action, decision or plan. It is the trigger or motivation behind an action, and produces goals, action or thinking. It can be negative or positive, and may be internal for a single person, or shared with a group or external market.

- **Intuits**: People who act moment-to-moment, often in a creative and fun way. They make decisions on gut responses and feelings. They seek freedom and influence others' moods.

- **Inventory**: A unique set of skills, knowledge and experiences that reinforce your unique approach and enhance your brand.

- **Language barrier**: The jargon and set of specialized words used to differentiate or define a situation, often unique to an industry, domain or company. It is a barrier to entry for people not in the group, and a way to determine if a person is capable in a specific domain. It can be used to gain access and build trust.

- **Market identity**: The sum of what you present to your target audience, both visually and verbally.

- **Market position**: How a brand differentiates itself within its sector, compared to its competitors.

- **Marketing**: Actions, systems and tools used to establish a particular offer or message in the minds of a target audience without direct conversations. See also: sales.

- **Negative feedback**: Information from the market about the areas that customers believe the brand can improve. A learning and modification tool.

- **Offer**: A promise to the future; a manifestation of your intention. It is shown through language, which describes how you provide a solution to someone's concern or problem. It's what you claim to do or deliver and its value to your market.

- **Passion**: A domain you want to focus on, driven by a willingness to suffer or sacrifice to gain additional knowledge, skill or experience in this domain.

- **Personal brand**: A personal identity that stimulates a meaningful emotional response in another person or audience about the values and qualities for which you stand. This is what others think of when they think of you.

- **Priority contacts**: A list of the most important people who you want to make aware of your offer.

- **Referrals**: A situation where someone recommends another person or product to another person, in most cases without financial gain. A badge of credibility.

- **Relationship business**: When the market cannot differentiate between similar products or services, it defaults to working with individuals who they know or like.

- **Sales**: (also called direct selling) Direct contact and interaction with the target customer or client, used to persuade them to purchase a product or service. *See also: marketing.*

- **Self-discovery**: A process of uncovering your unique approach, passions and inventory, leading to a clear sense of what you can uniquely offer to the market.

- **Selfish benefit**: What people want for themselves in a given situation: this might be their primary concern (such as freedom, certainty or safety), or the way they want things to be.

- **Strategic neglect**: A decision to de-prioritize or stop doing actions, so that time and energy can be applied to more valuable opportunities.

- **System**: A set of processes, actions and behaviors you put in place to achieve an intended result.

- **Theme**: Words that describe your approach that form a clear, consistent and unified message.

- **Thinkers**: People who want to direct situations; they want to be certain that results are as they planned and predicted. They often want to be right and to be in control, so they spend a substantial amount of time thinking about how to achieve this.

- **Value conversation**: A method of establishing or calculating the worth of a specific result, as measured by money or time. See also: benefit.

- **Value proposition**: What you are proposing to produce for your target market, in terms of time and/or money.

- **WIIFM**: An abbreviation for "What's in it for me?" This is a phrase clients might think when they are told about a product or service; before they consider buying, they will evaluate its selfish benefit.

Acknowledgments

I have many people to be thankful for, because they helped me bring this book to life. I want to first thank my wife, Mary Robbins, for her endless support and encouragement. She sparked the idea to turn the Atomic Branding portion of my coaching practice into this book.

My mom, Helen Robbins, set me on the path of creating my identity, and has always helped me to realize my true, authentic self.

John Cundiff and Travis Carson taught me to build a career based on using what comes out of me effortlessly for the benefit of others. Tim O'Brien helped me think about systems for personal branding.

My longtime colleague and collaborator, Katherine Steen, was instrumental in building a structure for the material in this book. Jo Buckman helped me find my voice and commit the first (of many!) drafts to paper.

Heidi Joy Tretheway provided the developmental and line edits that were the collaboration I needed to polish and publish. She also offered design and publishing guidance. Cynthia Moyer provided proofreading and formatting support.

Lastly, I'm grateful to the colleagues and clients — who I also count as dear friends — who put up with late-night inquiries about their personal brands, and generously cheered me on thoughout my career.

About the author

Craig Robbins is a business performance coach and founder of Next Level Business Career Coaching. His goal is to create space for clients — people, teams, and organizations — to go to the next level and generate a sustainable competitive advantage.

Past clients include General Electric, Coca-Cola, Colliers International, City of Hope, CBRE, Mutual of Omaha, Marsh McLennan, Trinity Capital, Kamehameha Schools, and a wide array of businesses and professionals. He has trained people from more than 60 countries, in industries including commercial real estate, technology, medicine, law, finance, development, magazines, insurance, retail, family trusts, and institutions. To learn more about Craig's coaching practice, please visit: CraigRobbinsNextLevel.com.

Prior to coaching, Craig served as Global COO and Chief Knowledge Officer at Colliers International, and Senior Vice President and Regional Manager at CBRE, both top global commercial real estate firms. Craig was also involved with founding Loopnet, the leading commercial real estate internet company, and served as Vice President of Products and Services.

Craig holds a degree in economics from UCLA and completed post-graduate work at MIT and Harvard. In 2002, Craig carried the torch in the Olympics.

Craig and Mary, his wife of 33 years, live in La Cañada, California. In his spare time, Craig enjoys fitness and all things next level, including becoming an award-winning brewer with Hilltop Brewers, where their Kolsch won second place nationally.

Made in the USA
Monee, IL
11 April 2024

56419681R00125